ATTRACTION SELLING

*Unleashing The Law Of Attraction
To Multiply Sales Results With Music,
Sleep, And The Justin Michael Method 3.0*

JUSTIN MICHAEL

JONES MEDIA
PUBLISHING

Jones Media Publishing
10645 N. Tatum Blvd. Ste. 200-166
Phoenix, AZ 85028
JonesMediaPublishing.com

Printed in the United States of America

ISBN: 978-1-948382-81-6 paperback
12 11 10 9 8 7 6 5 4 3 2 1

Ready to multiply your sales results?

G et all the resources and bonus material for this book and the JMM series in one place.

Download the book resources here free:
SalesSuperpowers.com/bonus

To my better half – Thank you for seeing
my brilliance even when I couldn't.
I love you.

TABLE OF CONTENTS

Metamorphosis

*"We are not human beings having a spiritual experience.
We are spiritual beings having a human experience."*

– *Pierre Teilhard de Chardin*

How do you feel right now? That's the great secret—feelings are the cosmic rudder of your "human body" ship voyaging through the multiverse, plotting your course amongst the stars in the illusion of a space-time continuum. What if there were infinite parallel universes, as Stephen Webb postulates in his book covering seventy-five solutions to the Fermi paradox? What if you had the endless potential to achieve any goal or dream in the same way that gravitational fields can seem to penetrate between multiverses living on the branes in the fourth dimension, where universes are mere millimeters away?

Whatever you're feeling deep down is what you will attract.

Why it's that way is a mystery to so many of us. As we get older – yes, over the age of 7 – our feelings become chronic. We give a litany of excuses as to why life isn't the way we want it, unwitting victims of past trauma we re-experience outside of our waking awareness. We beat ourselves up emotionally. We often live lives of quiet desperation in fear, secretly hating ourselves in guilt, blame, shame, and regret. And if you choose "sales" for a living and do it right, it's one of the most rejection-dense, brutal professions you can endure, with stratospheric highs and ultra-low lows.

You have to get your mind right to thrive and survive. Especially if you want to OPEN, progress, and CLOSE deals with enthusiasm and consistency.

That said, sales is the best profession in the world. You can come from nothing, make unlimited income, achieve financial freedom, and have a lifestyle you could only dream of. But that's only about 1% of executives, coaches, consultants, and entrepreneurs. You'll need a new mindset and skills to thrive in this cutthroat profession.

I've delivered a veritable horn of plenty of my sales secrets to you in the last two books, but there's still something missing.

Only 5% of our waking lives stem from our conscious mind. Most of us can't see what's blocking us, even if we're in therapy or recovery, and optimistically set solid goals and New Year's resolutions. Still, we plateau and move laterally (check-to-check) for decades, wishing we could achieve more: greater purpose, meaning, results, joy, and fulfillment in our lives.

The repetition kills many of us, causing burnout, and many give up and quit sales before they find the silver lining: *service*. Authentic selling is giving and helping others transform their businesses and lives to achieve a far better state by assertively introducing quality products and services with real ROI.

"Seek happiness from within, rather than chasing it externally." – Wayne Dyer

Life is costly in our modern world. We earn more yearly but amass more debt faster from retail therapy, cosmetic surgery, healthcare, or lingering student and personal debt. We want to be younger, richer, more intelligent, and fitter – anything but accepting who we are.

The hedonic treadmill: the more we make, the more we consume. Greed and envy cause many of us to implode. The irony is winning the game of life the opposite of that: radical self-acceptance is the doorway to everything good.

But they don't teach you in school that you can instantly change your state, self-perception, and mental chatter, creating a new world with unlimited potential. You can access infinite parallel universes in real time, tapping into the power of your positive thoughts to reprogram your subconscious mind.

Everyone is searching for an answer in the future or the past, but if you can slow down enough, you can find it hidden within the stillness of the here and now: inside yourself all along.

> *"Always say 'yes' to the present moment. What could be more futile, more insane, than to create inner resistance to what already is? What could be more insane than to oppose life itself, which is now and always now? Surrender to what is. Say 'yes' to life – and see how life suddenly starts working for you rather than against you." – Eckhart Tolle*

My advice may be highly contrastive to your future, which feels like a swarm of bees about to sting you. I've gone through the bottom of this life only to rise again like a phoenix from the ashes. I can attest that these statements are 100% true. I was surprised I made it to 30 or earned $100K (not to mention seven figures). Using what's in this book, I finally built my self-esteem to an incredible place through serving. I don't even recognize myself from 20 years ago when the story started. To paraphrase Maxwell Maltz, "You can get a facelift, but the internal scars usually remain."

"Our self-image, strongly held, essentially determines what we become." – Maxwell Maltz

And now I will help you go from the gutter to the stars even if things feel grim but may look shiny outwardly as they did for me. I went from average rep getting by to a well-respected top VP of SaaS sales, earning half a million a year within five years of figuring this out.

So, let's discuss and demystify a controversial subject:

Miracles.

That's what this mighty little book is ultimately about. Not only creating them but *being* them.

I've seen inexplicable miracles come into my life and that of those I've coached by applying the simple principles herein. Fusing the law of attraction, sales methodology, music, visualization, and sleep in a radical new blend will change your world.

It all started with a secret paper I wrote in 2011 called *Musifestation. You can get a copy for free with the book bonuses at SalesSuperPowers.com/bonus.*

I was at my wit's end, willing to do almost anything to get hired in Silicon Valley's red ocean—cue the Will Smith cold-calling scene from *Pursuit of Happyness.*

Fast forward twelve years, and my process has worked unanimously for my clients. I've worked with hundreds and hundreds of them to change their limiting beliefs and improve their self-image. Shattering their income ceiling and often 5Xing their earnings, I've helped them unabashedly move up in the world with a new identity, sense of pride, and vastly improved skill set in a very short period relative to their life span.

Music is the first missing ingredient to unlocking the law of attraction. I've even seen it create focus and ease the burden of a client's head trauma from a car accident. I'm so proud he's pursuing his dreams despite this setback that would paralyze most people. We find new strength in the broken places.

Whether you know it or not, you are a miracle and creator of miracles.

When this transformative information found me, I shone brightly on the surface. But the reality was I was down and out, living in a loft check-to-check, raising money for charity on a wing and a prayer, living an unhealthy lifestyle both mentally and physically, without a clue about business or life now that I look back on it.

I believed I'd failed as a musician and producer and was just going through the motions to eke out a living selling. I hadn't even read a single sales book, not to mention getting a clue I'd one day be a bestselling "sales" author.

I was skeptical and jaded and had a very stubborn fixed mindset. I was faking it and not making it. Resentment and vindictiveness were my MO (modus operandi)—excuses, blame, and abusing my mind and body daily and nightly.

But somewhere deep down, I still wanted to make something of myself. Many people believed in me and saw greatness, like my mother, father, and early mentors, even when I couldn't.

Not only was I failing consistently, but I had long since given up believing I'd succeed at anything in life, no less financially or in business. Most of my time was dedicated to art and music, just trying to go against the grain. Groucho Marx nailed it, "I refuse to join any club that would have me as a member."

Can you relate? So, I fell into software sales without a degree and much ambition, chasing my brother up to San Francisco, an engineer at Google. But even he didn't want to help me get a job as I'd burned that bridge. I started telemarketing when I was 21 and had a friend who was an entrepreneur in e-education, so I began to pick up some guerilla marketing and social media work in SoCal incubators while couch surfing by age 26.

The beginning of this story is literally that humble. One fine day in my mid-twenties, I remember having next to nothing and floating in the Pacific Ocean with my entrepreneur friend Patrick, telling him, "Maybe I should take what I did for bands on Myspace and port that over to marketing and sales for tech companies." I had once amassed 200,000+ followers there, which meant something back in 2004.

But what's wildly ironic going from the gutter to the stars is that I'm way more humble now. That's the rare quality I admire most in a tiny percentage of successful people: they never forget where they came from. I can't stand it when people "big time" the youth. Stevie Wonder once spent a half hour with me when I was only 19 for no reason in his rehearsal hall and taught me by example not only what real genius is but how caring about one person can lead to a life where millions show up at your funeral.

I have no regrets because it was worth every scar, lesson, six-figure mistake, and friend lost to become the person I am today. I gained real street smarts and an uncanny ability to read people (which would help me immeasurably later in selling) based on meeting stadiums full, selling shoes part-time, and running the door at a venue.

Once, a billionaire, maybe it was Paul Orfalea, confirmed this statement to me, which I rejected as a cliché, "It's not about making millions; it's about the person you become in the process of doing it." And it turns out it's a cliché for a reason. Success changes you. Paul was always generous with his time in those halcyon "before" days when I naively believed I'd figured life out.

Success breeds more successes until your life is an upward spiral and positive snowball called "winning." But that payout is a total reflection of an inner game, a silent victory. Some of the poorest humans *seem* rich, outwardly hiding hollow shells, choking out the abundance of this earthly paradise we live in with evil intentions and self-doubt. Envy, not greed, is "driving the world," Charlie Munger [RIP] hit the nail on the head.

I didn't stand a snowball's chance of breaking through in my mid-twenties.

But I wanted to do good things in the world. I still had a heart of gold. I needed to stop pretending to be David Copperfield and learn to become the true me without the smoke and mirrors. Self-mastery is where the real magic begins.

I've shown you every last sales secret and hack in the previous two *JMM*™ series books. You know how I generated an avalanche of new business via prospecting innovation. But this book solves a more significant problem: *you are getting in your own way.*

At 31, I finally snapped. I changed my mindset. I refused to fail. A voice inside me grew louder, saying, "You deserve better. Expect more for yourself." So, I moved to SF from LA. I networked. I never gave up. I created my lucky break in the physical universe, but it started in my mind. I remembered triumphal times when I was a straight-A student at 15 or won the school talent show. I reached down and found the next gear despite a situation that looked quite bleak at the time.

Showing up in Silicon Valley without a college degree or SaaS experience led to 5,000 doors getting shut hard in my face – literally! After three months of searching for roles, they offered me the same $45K base I made in SoCal. My brother pissed me off to no end when he encouraged me, "Take the job and move up; it's the best you can do."

But I refused and used the process of *Musifestation* and got an offer at $95K that led me to make $115K that next year. The days were long, getting up before dawn and riding Caltrain from Palo Alto into SF, but the payoff of knowledge and upskilling was sweet. The 2-hour daily commute and 8-hour work days gave me time to think, research, read books about the mind, and sell like crazy.

I finally started to live up to my potential, master my emotions, and understand where I was heading. I worked like I had a gun to my head, first one in, last one to leave, but it was my big break, and I wouldn't miss the chance to optimize it.

I always say: *from acorns, oaks.*

Wherever you are in your life: if you're broke, sick, in debt, frustrated, suffering, questioning yourself, or even ready to quit sales, this book will plant the seed to change all that. Recently, a client called me up and said working with me had so inspired him he decided not to contemplate taking his own life.

God's gift is to encourage someone at the most profound level. While many see suicide as a selfish act, he's a superhero in my eyes for facing down his demons and learning to love himself at long last. In the time spent with me, he created an opening, a possibility for change. It's never too late to begin creating the life you want.

From a client just now: "I was just talking to my wife about some of the stuff I've been doing recently, and I said, 'It's like I'm starting to develop superpowers,' and then realized that's what you called your book."

Saving lives and creating superheroes is not what I set out to do. I set out to simply *give*. I realized in these 44 years that inner peace, happiness, and joy inextricably tie in with service, love, and giving. If you don't completely do this for yourself, you cannot do it for others: that's the paradox. But what I get to do now is so powerful I cherish it.

Coaching is a bizarre profession where you make your own rules. For those interested in creating a side hustle to do what I do, please realize that your ability to serve others powerfully is only limited by the "health of the healer." (hat tip, Steve Chandler) You can only take others so far as you've taken yourself.

It's not just my passion to help sales leaders, founders, coaches, and consultants who struggle like I used to find their true purpose and connect to their higher self (and hey, I'm still not perfect); it's my mission on this planet. It raises vibration. More people get help. The ripple effect of paying it forward creates a better world. Based on the title, you probably thought you would read another "power of positive thinking" sales "pump-up" book to become a "quota crusher." Still, the material we will tackle is so much more profound and transformational than that.

You're infinitely powerful—each of you. And I'm going to prove it to you.

You probably don't believe me. I never thought this way. Maybe you're about to put this thing down in disgust. More BS! Ugh. Like all my books, I'll repurchase it if it doesn't completely transform your life.

Hard talk time:

Failure: it's why you're here. It's why you bought yet another book on the law of attraction. You've heard it all before. A *JMM*™ book about this may give you a faint sense of *hope*. Your thoughts determine your reality, which is the mantra we have all lived by.

But somehow, all your attempts at positive thinking, visualization, meditation, chants, and spiritual practices bring the same, even *less* abundant, sales and business opportunities into your life. "This stuff doesn't work," we've all thought frustratedly, ingesting another airport self-help book like stale in-flight cookies, abandoning it ten pages later. Why? Being.

Being = your identity

You're not getting what you truly want in this life and your career because you haven't shifted *who* you fundamentally are. Let's get to the heart of the issue now, pulling no punches. I was selfish, and therefore, I was blocking my growth. I lacked gratitude and took God's blessings for granted. I was choking out abundance and prosperity, my birthright, from flowing into my life. And karma was a double-edged sword until I began to live by this quote:

> *"When you are able to shift your inner awareness to how you can serve others, and when you make this the central focus of your life, you will then be in a position to know true miracles in your progress toward prosperity." – Wayne W. Dyer [RIP]*

You're here because you truly want your life to change. You've maintained the status quo for years, the exact identity for decades. Heck, probably since you were seven years old. You are probably in sales of some kind, aren't we all? But a voice inside you says, "I'm not good enough." You have impostor syndrome. You fear failure; maybe you even fear success.

"You can never get enough of what you don't want," Wayne Dyer said. But why is that? Because your reality is the sum of all dreams and fears. Because you subconsciously attract the exact income you believe you can make beyond your awareness. Have you ever stopped to realize that? When I did, it floored me. I did $300K+ one year and owed $35K in debt; how could that be?

The more you make, the more you spend to keep up with the Joneses (hedonic treadmill), and your comfort zone created over years of chronic poor thinking keeps you in a Goldilocks zone or homeostasis, relegating you to the same level of experience. (hedonic adaptation) Hence, 70% of lottery winners go bankrupt. We've all had that friend who dates the same crazy person repeatedly: cyclical manifestation, karma, or the law of attraction.

The good news is, I was once like you in some iteration. I was once 26 years old with a death wish. As I see it now, in many ways, by my 20s, I'd already given up on life. I was in a headspace below death because I didn't care about mortality or think my actions had any consequences. Did that make me a bad person, or was it just faithless apathy? Maybe a combination of both. But people saw greatness in me when I couldn't muster the courage to see it in myself.

Earning $45K a year and supervising an outsourced sales team in Costa Rica and the Philippines of 1,000 telemarketers with bodyguards in tow blinded me. My CFO told me once, "Justin, if you ever realize what you've got, you'll be a millionaire overnight."

Another angel in the wings was Jackson Browne's CPA, as I randomly threw a concert promotion for his singer-songwriter daughter at the venue I ran, which Mariah Carey's first producer built.

Only some people plot to do you in. Angels are waiting in the wings. And so, as a thank you, I was randomly introduced to Jack Canfield from *Chicken Soup for the Soul* fame at a benefit, and my first snarky response to him was, "Oh yeah, my 10th-grade English teacher, Dave, made us read your book." Then I felt like an idiot when I realized what a monster self-help guru he is with *The Success Principles*. Stunned, I reviewed all his books and tapes I won at the charity auction.

That was me, 26, green and clueless, with a massive basket of his stuff, listening to his audio day and night in my Toyota Corolla. At the same time, I promoted random touring artist showcases like the unknown Katy Perry, and once, Jack Johnson and David Crosby even attended my shows. It was a running start.

Jack Canfield handed me this little black plastic DVD case and mentioned casually, "Hey, this is something I want you to check out that hasn't been released to the public yet. It's called *The Secret*." Within six weeks, I met Rhonda Byrne through bizarre synchronistic events, discovering Wallace Wattles and *The Science of Getting Rich (1910)*.

I must have read that book over 1,000 times over the next five years and ended up, after about a 15-year time delay, achieving and exceeding every last dream I had for myself. I shattered my income ceiling and 10X'd most goals I never thought I could achieve. But we'll get into it later.

At that moment, I thought, "Well, here's this world-famous author, and I'd like to see what I could gain in a soundbite asking one burning question." I asked Jack, "What's the secret to event promotion?" Back then, I threw full-moon charity masquerade balls on rooftops for underprivileged kids. I am paraphrasing, but this is how I remember it, and it stopped me right in my tracks:

> *"The whole industry is spending trillions on building bigger, better, faster nets. You need to build a garden that attracts butterflies."*

That quote changed my life and is in Codex 1. You can get this codex in the bonus material for this book at SalesSuperpowers. com/bonus.

You are that garden. I've figured it out after everything I've done and learned these 18 years since that fateful day. You must cultivate your garden, weed your mind, and love yourself. You must attract the butterflies: your clients and customers. You must shift polarity via curiosity so they chase you.

You can pull all the resources, people, and experiences toward you. YOU are the ultimate prize. Oren Klaff calls this one a "prize frame." But it's more fundamental: you are the "prize" because you have a heart of gold and all the value in the world to offer. Only you can convince yourself otherwise.

Once you realize this fact, you become unstoppable.

That's the essence of what coaching is to me. I see the pure gold in people and help them see it, too. Then, they transform, tapping into their unique genius and stepping into their power.

And like a butterfly, you will go through a metamorphosis from the pages of this book. Because the answers you've been looking for your whole life are standing right there in front of you, staring you in the face. When was the last time you looked in the mirror into your eyes and witnessed the miracle of an iris? The mere construction of a human eye is so complex, miraculous, and awe-inspiring that in an instant, we're filled with a sense of wonder like a child again.

People I work with 2-5X their income and get promoted within six months over and over. They shift something so much more fundamental than surface-level tactics or positive thinking. They reset and transform their very *being* through the *JMM*™ techniques.

> *"Tripled my income, just got promoted to AE, hiring SDRs, and building GTM strategy for incoming starters. JMM for life!" – Stephen McLeod*

Back to *Musifestation* and the origins of this work: I wrote it when I moved to Silicon Valley in 2011. I couldn't get a job for three months, having quit one that paid me only $45K. I had no college degree, which gave me a massive chip on my shoulder and little software as a service (SaaS) skill or experience. Recruiters told me to "lie on your resume" and put "some college."

At the time, I was very deep on Neville Goddard and all the neo-transcendentalist writers from the turn of the century, like W. Clement Stone (Jack's mentor), Napoleon Hill, Ralph Waldo Emerson, and Johann Wolfgang von Goethe, who influenced Rhonda's journey in *The Secret*. In our time by her roaring fire, I thumbed through the pages of close-ups of the Sistine Chapel, and I thought about Michelangelo's inhuman levels of dedication hanging from the ceiling painting on his back for years perfecting it. What if I gave that kind of devotion to my art and life?

She told me the secret behind the secret is *giving*: to "want your dreams for others" even more than yourself. I think that's why tithing and philanthropy work.

She explained the most potent exercise is giving with so much love you have tears in your eyes. She recalled how she'd emptied her ATM and started walking down the streets in Australia, giving out bills and thanking people with the deepest possible gratitude in her heart. We all know what happened next: 30 million copies sold, translation into 50 languages, and grossing $300 million dollars.

The lesson: If you focus the superpowers you gain in this book on enriching yourself, it unleashes a curse like the explorers who sought out the Holy Grail, "Lost City of Gold," or Ponce De León's quest for the "Fountain of Youth."

The other *secret behind the secret* is taking massive 10X action. Lewis Howes pointed out, "Action is in the word attraction."

But the most profoundly overlooked realm is GIVING. What you intend for others, you get. Listen to Zig Ziglar's immortal words, "You can have everything in life you want if you just help other people get what they want."

Another time I ran into her, she quizzed me, "What was the longest chapter of Wattles?" I smiled, "Gratitude." Rhonda adds, "Gratitude is the great multiplier. Set the universal forces in your favor. Whatever you are grateful and thankful for multiplies."

I memorized *The Science of Getting Rich* and lived its pages for thousands of reads, practicing it daily for years. It's in the public domain, so I suggest you read it now. You can get through it in one sitting.

Synthesizing all of this and applying it to software sales was step one. There are roughly 11MM software sellers and a mind-blowing 400 million small business owners who are the engines of the global economy. They desperately need the knowledge of sales and LOA to be fused.

What happened to me over the last 18 years is nothing short of a miracle, kind of insane, and beyond my wildest dreams, like *Mr. Toad's Wild Ride.* Now, *you* are about to embark on an incredible adventure from the Shire and over the Misty Mountains to slay your inner dragons. "Where we're going, we don't need roads," Doc Brown proclaims before flooring his time-traveling DeLorean *Back to the Future.* But be careful: the destination is way outside of your comfort zone. Why do you think they call them "growing pains."

We will time travel to your best version of the future and teleport it back into the present, experiencing it repeatedly until it's a foregone conclusion in your psyche, a self-fulfilling prophecy. Your journey will be nonlinear, just like mine: exponential growth.

I moved from a $45K per year rep to bidding wars with top startups fighting to pay me $200-250K base and $500K+ OTE. Within five years of touching down in the Valley, I elevated myself to VP, RVP, VP Ops, and GM, and then VCs invested $3MM, mapping my brain into an AI.

I won an Elon Musk-inspired *10X Award* for "relentless resourcefulness" from a Tier-1 VC-backed Seattle startup with an 80MM run rate for generating six years of pipeline in 6 months. I remember how surreal it felt standing up to receive it in front of 350+ global employees in 6 countries.

I thought, "Damn, I have arrived." But that was just the beginning: Silicon Valley came knocking within six months. Ben Sardella, who co-founded Datanyze (acquired by ZoomInfo), and Bryan Franklin, Reid Hoffman's business coach, were looking for the top SDR in the world to build a new autonomous prospecting model with engineers.

Sound familiar? If you think about how ChatGPT and OpenAI only recently emerged, we were far ahead of our time in 2017. AI-based personalization via sentence injection into 32 custom fields was the only way, thanks to our visionary CTO Anders Fredriksson.

For that whole story, read my first international bestseller, *Tech-Powered Sales*, which I wrote with Tony J. Hughes in 2020. Jones Media published this book series you're reading now, which became an instant bestseller. Although initially turned down by six publishers because of its metaphysical nature, my follow-up *JMM*™ series to *TPS* has continued to sell at the pace of *GAP Selling*.

I am now a 5X published author and have earned millions in consulting. The battle-tested techniques I've developed and taught have driven over 1B in revenue for thousands of executives worldwide.

I remember an affirmation Jack Canfield used to say, and it seemed really over the top back then. "I am a genius and apply my wisdom." Another early mentor, Ron, used to say, "Justin, your genius is communication." I'd laugh and reply, "OK, Ron, so what you're saying is, I'll be broke." Ron used to sweep the floor of a plastics factory he later would run, so I was paying attention. I just couldn't translate that gift into a way to monetize.

These days, I help people take that mental leap often, finding and harnessing their unique genius.

I have been on a mission to revolutionize outbound prospecting methodology for the past eight years. Thanks to my mentor Tony Hughes's *Combo Prospecting*, which featured me as the case study, I have challenged the core mechanics of the traditional client acquisition approach and created what many consider the most profound and practical, tactical outbound operating system for generating predictable revenue.

Because I believed in the possibility of that genius, I thought I could be "great." I felt I was creating "that garden" within my mind and soul. I *attracted* the butterflies.

Rejected by tech companies 5,000 times, like in the movie *Rudy,* where he's finally accepted to play football for Notre Dame, I made it to Salesforce and LinkedIn at the Empire State Building with no college degree.

Wherever you read this, I know what you're thinking: "Great, another overprivileged dude who read *The Secret*." No, quite the contrary. I lived it.

I studied the *Law of Attraction* back to its origins in Hermetic traditions and ancient Egypt, peeling back the onion on psychoanalysis, *Psycho-Cybernetics, Three Principles,* and Syd Banks, the "being trinity" of Chandler-Hardison-Litvin, Bob Proctor, Werner Erhard, Brené Brown, Wayne Dyer, Dr. Joe Dispenza, Eckhart Tolle, Byron Katie, Tony Robbins's "priming," neuro-linguistic programming colloquially known as NLP, *Silva Mind Control*, Cialdini persuasion, Dr. Joseph Murphy, game theory, relationship dynamics (á la Neil Strauss), military strategy, *The Tools* by Phil Stutz, and the collective works of luminary synthesizers like Dr. Benjamin Hardy, Ph.D. in organizational psychology.

The list goes for a country mile and meanders through vast and seemingly different content, making the journey longer.

Rather than questioning my sources and making this a hefty research project, this book is for people who want immediate results: increased sales, promotion, wealth, trips to President's Club, and living their mission in the world.

You can and will *be* MASSIVE with what I share and the exercises herein. You will immediately start to create miracles in your life. Take these counterintuitive, even controversial ideas on faith because I did; therefore, you can. Borderline religious, spiritual, and metaphysical, rest assured they are quantum mechanics-based. Still, the origin is less important than the fact that the processes always work if applied literally, like gravity.

> *"It is not uncommon for people to spend their whole life waiting to start living." – Eckhart Tolle*

Your life has already changed just by changing your perspective while reading this. For many of you, it's a shot in the arm and a reminder to conquer your greatest fear.

Don't "die with your music still inside you."

Wayne Dyer and Abraham Maslow superbly captured the purpose of our lives in that quote: self-actualization. For 20 years, I was terrified of not living up to my potential, and that's the number one thing I hear from my clients, who are often high performers. They want to side hustle but put it off another year. They want to become financially free but feel trapped and beholden to their robot overlords.

Despite all these outstanding accomplishments, when I turned 40, I realized I still hadn't released "my real music." I cut the cord on corporate life, launched my consultancy, and serendipitously met Julia Nimchinski, a genius entrepreneur and the Steve Jobs of B2B, co-founding several ambitious ventures like HYPCCCYCL (#2 GTM Community), Nimchinski/Michael (GTM Agency working with billion-dollar unicorn clients), and Hard Skill Exchange (world's 1st ever live 1:1 skill-building marketplace platform).

I thought, "If you want to take the island, burn the boats!" I was surprised to find it wasn't Tony Robbins who said that first; it was Julius Caesar. Am I going to spend the rest of my life working for Evil Mega Corp, making them 10s of millions of dollars, or burn the ships and work for myself? In other words, if I could only choose one entity to enrich for the rest of my life, would it be others or Justin Michael Inc.? Of course, I chose myself. You *must* choose yourself.

Do you work for others now? Don't worry, learn all you can. You will choose yourself eventually, even if you learn to master the craft from someone else at the moment.

And from that Joseph Campbell cave I feared to enter, all the gold and treasure I sought were waiting. But they'd always been there, I realized.

I coach people to fundamentally shift and transform their identity and subconscious mind to manifest a new life and result in business, health, wealth, relationships, and communion with a higher power. I help sales leaders immediately spin up an additional $5-20K per month side hustle.

I can play you video testimonials where an exec like Mike has tears in his eyes from the sudden prosperity, abundance, and joy he has now realized by 4Xing his income just because we met. He invested a handsome but fractional amount compared to the hundreds of thousands he made back and millions more he'll make with the *JMM*™ in his lifetime.

That's my *why*. This book is my gift back to the universe and the legions of sellers who have read my work these last eight years. I've put out a half dozen books and 17 open-source *Codex* guides (dropped to Reddit) while co-creating multiple communities across Discord, WhatsApp, and Slack to *pay it forward*.

> *"One must have chaos in oneself to give birth to a dancing star." – Friedrich Nietzsche*

Take the wisdom from my 20 years of failing forward navigating chaos: 20K hours on the phones, 5MM emails sent and A/B tested, 50 hours a week on LinkedIn for 15 years, spending millions (of my own and VC $) in making go-to-market mistakes and finding streaks, building up agencies from 10 clients to 100 concurrent, pushing 200+ ventures past their first (or next) ten million dollars of annual recurring revenue (ARR), and coaching 1,000+ reps.

Know this startling truth:

> *Our subconscious mind dictates 95% of our lives.*
>
> *Over 90% of our success comes directly from our self-image and mindset.*

A potential recruiter client once said, "I don't have a mindset problem. I make $150K a year." I responded, "You live in Dubai; that won't cut it. You *do* have a mindset problem." Then he wired me my fee.

We are all connected energetically. You can't fail if you do what I'm about to advise you. Let's get moving!

I want to thank Mendy Zimmerman, who's read a thousand books but took the time to re-read and help edit mine. He's a veritable badass at Midjourney prompting, too.

And I'll close this chapter with a testimonial: Eric *"Now"* Nowoslawski came my way inbound from Reddit after working for Cardone, and now he's doing webinars with Hormozi. I knew him when.

"Justin's coaching changed my life. It's like going to a real college. He doesn't necessarily teach you in-the-weeds stuff. He teaches you how to think differently about sales. I owe that guy my whole business right now. Take what he teaches you seriously; it will have a huge ROI. I went into debt but made it back and more because of his training. He put me on the path to running my agency. His ROI for me is higher than Bitcoin after 2012."

CHAPTER 1

Be-Do-Have Paradox (Action)

"Money doesn't bring happiness, but happiness brings money."

— Rhonda Byrne

Everyone is trying to *have* things. They mistakenly think people will trust and buy from them if they have the proper certification or badge on their profile. Suppose they drive the right car or wear the right watch. If they get fit, get surgery, and look a certain way, eventually, they will become extraordinary by looking the part.

"Fake it 'til you make it" has become the defining meme of our culture. Have it before you do it. Just put it on a credit card before you earn it. Even logically, do enough, and you'll *become* it. But how many people with an extremely high work ethic do we know who are still broke? These paths are outwardly seeking and cause even more emptiness inside.

I lived by this quote by Calvin Coolidge (the 30th US President), but it was not enough:

> *"Nothing in the world can take the place of persistence. Talent will not; nothing is more common than unsuccessful men with talent. Genius will not; unrewarded genius is almost a proverb. Education will not; the world is full of educated derelicts."*

Endless trillions get poured into sowing the seeds of dissatisfaction and malcontent that fuel the constant pursuit of status. One dopamine hit after another, the tech companies are brain-hacking you at 250 alerts per day.

> *"If you are not paying for it, you're not the customer; you're the product being sold." – Andrew Lewis*

That's outward and backward materialistic thinking. Bodies get old, decay, and die. We are spirits living in a material world. People only buy anything because of the "experience with the seller." Therefore, "people buy *you*" á la Jeb Blount. And that *you* is the inner you: presence and being.

If you think about it:

Do-Have-Be (wrong)

Have-Be-Do (wrong)

Be-Do-Have (truth)

Ultimately, these formulas fail because it's only possible to *BE* someone different (identity shift), which changes your thoughts; your actions follow, and then you create a new outcome. That's how you break the cycle of Einstein's definition of insanity: "doing the same thing you always did and expecting different results."

I recently put up a poll with this chicken and egg problem: What's the most crucial factor to double your income? Execution or mindset. The results split down the middle on nearly 300 votes. But the crowd agreed: you can't execute until you get your mind right. Some commented, "Well, isn't any execution better than solely a changed mindset?" And that's where people who missed the boat on the original law of attraction run amok.

> *"If you have built castles in the air, your work need not be lost; there is where they should be. Now put foundations under them." – Henry David Thoreau*

Your subconscious mind is always driving everything, and what you suggest to it through your chronic thoughts dictates what you program it to do automatically under the surface of your waking reality. You and every billionaire have ±70,000 thoughts per day. According to the National Science Foundation, 80% of these are negative, and 95% are repetitive from the day before. Harvard Business Review cites various sources that we make 35,000 daily decisions to pursue happiness – will yours be negative or positive? While it sounds masochistic, it's so hard to change our subconscious mind because we've all become so addicted to the safety of habitual negative thinking.

Dr. Joe Dispenza shares these great nuggets with Jay Shetty (watch the whole YouTube interview): "A thought that you think over and over again becomes a belief. Nerve cells that fire together wire together. The process of change requires becoming conscious of your unconscious thoughts. Just because you have that thought doesn't mean it's the truth. The thought of 'being unworthy' produces the feeling of 'being unworthy,' which tends to cause a person to think more *unworthy* thoughts. If you confront that thought and make a different choice, get ready because you will feel uncomfortable."

Thoughts influence feelings, which influence your body's physiology, which leads to the same choices, producing more feelings and influencing your thoughts in a vicious cycle. Over millions of years, our survival instincts and self-protection mechanisms caused us to evolve our brains this way.

I'll let you in on a little secret that will open the doorway to freedom from a lifetime of suffering and beating yourself up inside: *It's not you!* It never has been. The default setting of humanity is not conducive to mental health. There's a very good chance there's nothing wrong with you.

It's time to break the cycle.

> *"Learn how to manifest your ideal reality by understanding and recoding your energetic field, as success is 80% internal reality and 20% external action."* – Regan Hillyer

Why are top sellers, celebrities, and billionaires more successful than you or me? Have you ever really wondered and unpacked this? It's simple.

One word: Self-belief.

Their internal concept of themselves and the self-image they built up over childhood or a lifetime of winning is extra solid. We know this to be true because when captains of industry lose everything, they often rebuild it rapidly. The offspring of Presidents are not always the finest humans but often end up rich. Chalk it up to nepotism, but again, it comes down to a higher level of self-belief. Growing up, they could do no wrong. Their parents pumped them up. "C- report card? What a genius."

In contrast, 70% of lottery winners lose everything, never to be gained again. It's a proverb. I'll explain the deeper reasons why.

So then, what holds us back? Childhood trauma, negativity, buying into the lie that traumatic experiences are our destiny - a story we can't change. We aren't our story. We just buy into that myth. Psychotherapy can help you sort yourself out, but it won't change the scars that become recurring automatic thoughts and chronic self-suggestions. We must develop a new addiction to habitual positive thinking and reverse the cycle to be reborn.

Realize you are not your thoughts, your mind, or your body.

You are the consciousness behind these connected to the universal mind, throwing the formless into form, relating to the one source, a higher power (or God), whatever your definition. If you are an atheist, just realize the power of your mind on the brain far exceeds all supercomputers combined. Your reticular activating systems (RAS) will deliver what you BELIEVE autonomously and precisely, throwing 100 billion neurons into motion.

From being, everything else springs eternal.

Who are you *being* in this moment? Are you confident? Are you the best at what you do? Do *you* believe you are capable of the nth degree? Most people must see concrete evidence of their ability before they are convinced. Lack of faith prevents them from achieving the very thing they want most. They remain powerless in life "at the effect" because they don't see the results of their power in reality. We must move from "effect" to "cause."

The paradox is: know that you are great. You will be great. Know that you are strong: you will be strong. Cultivate a healthy respect for your genius, and your genius will rapidly manifest. How can you become happy? Be happy now. Smile, and it's impossible to be depressed. In complete stillness of the body, it's impossible to exhibit anger by neuroscience law.

We become what we believe. If that's all you take away from this book, it's now priceless.

But I thought this was a book on sales and the law of attraction.

If you don't follow this formula, someone else with a higher self-belief coming from that frame will outperform you in this world. It's tough to get there. I can relate because I hated myself for so long for no apparent reason.

My parents believed in me growing up and only ever pushed me to do what I love. So they gave me the gift of self-motivation and pursuing passions that are not the almighty dollar alone. Figuring out how to earn a great living came far later, and maybe that's a journey of self-discovery we all have to embark on as it's "not taught."

And yet, I never consciously *chose* to be happy. I was always waiting for an elusive proof like a Grammy Award falling in my lap, allowing me to accept who I was and finally love myself. It ultimately robbed me of genuine gratitude and brought despair and misfortune until I figured this out. I had everything going for me except that I was permitting the monkey on my back to rule my life.

My thoughts were killing me.

We are going to attack your psyche, slaughter your ego, and start to reprogram your subconscious mind with this book through powerful suggestions: affirmations, visualization to music, I call *Musifestation*, and changing your identity frame with deep psychological processes, you can perform on yourself daily. Yoga, meditation, chanting, deep-tissue massage, prayer, and even hypnosis can help, but those aren't my specialties, so I'll leave you alone to explore those mysteries with other experts.

Relaxation links to mental and spiritual power, so seek it out in the interspaces of life wherever and whenever you can find it. Time is our most valuable commodity. We all get the same 24 hours in a day.

I've pulled these practical "mind control" techniques from every corner of history and philosophy, but these are the ones that work for me and have real-world results regarding manifestation. You can do them in 30 minutes per day.

Because so many people complain that I don't get into the meat of my books for a long build-up and intro, let's just get to the book's heart now.

"Sound is the medicine of the future." – Edgar Cayce

10 Proven Processes for Subconscious Transformation

1. AFFIRMATIONS:

We are what we believe. We are what we feel. We are what we know to be true. We are our *I AM*—first process. In many traditions, when God created the world, the first words spoken were *I AM*. So build a list of I AM statements and read them aloud to yourself twice daily in the mirror. Or, close your eyes and listen to Solfeggio-based 432Hz (connection to the universe, enhanced mental clarity and focus) or 528Hz music (DNA healing & miracles). Celebrate achieving your goals in advance! Pick the top 5 things you want in this life, say them every day over and over again, and jump for joy, literally (or in your mind, per Rhonda Byrne).

YouTube and Spotify have a million channels dedicated to this, so just do a quick search. Google "All 9 Solfeggio Frequencies," "Crystal Singing Bowls," and Gregorian or Tibetan "Om" chants. Make sure it's played in specially-tuned hertz frequencies – never 440Hz. These scales cymatically* rearrange your DNA and create harmony across your chakras, cleansing auras. Remember: your body is a toroidal energy field radiating approximately 2-5 feet on all sides. *Cymatics is the "study of visible sound." Look into it; we will dive way deeper later.*

2. VISUALIZATION-Musifestation (music + meditation = manifestation):

Process two: Reframe your identity. Believe in the new you, get into the emotion, holographically experience the feeling of *your wishes fulfilled* (Dyer/Goddard), and seek evidence in the real world that it already happened for you exactly as you expect it to appear. But be patient!

When you set this vision to sacred music and repeat it 2x per day, it's even more powerful. The modern 440Hz scale is controversial, but rather than get into its conspiracy theory origin story, just look at footage of the impact of sound waves on water or sand on a metal plate when playing ancient frequencies pointed at it. Beautifully complex geometric shapes appear.

That's what it's doing to your brainwaves and DNA - tuning them for positive resonance and energetic alignment with the universe. Specific sonic frequencies like 528Hz open the heart chakra and align with light waves, in this case toward the middle of the visible spectrum. That sound wave goes with the color green we see everywhere in pristine nature on our lush planet. Forests and trees emit it.

It's all connected: color can also heal. It's well known today that various combinations of sound and color can be therapeutic. Study the chromatic spectrum and the linkages between sonic and electromagnetic waves. While sound is carried in the air, light travels through the vacuum via always-on electromagnetic fields. They are both oscillations, so the implications are bidirectional. Your mind and thoughts emit energy and frequencies that impact these fields, which can, in return, impact you.

Creating harmony with specially tuned music that makes you relax like Binaural beats allows you to get into an alpha or theta brainwave state (vs. our usual Beta "high focus") where it's much easier to program the subconscious.

Binaural beats are a perception of sound created by your brain. If you listen to two tones, each at a different frequency and each in a different ear, your brain creates an additional tone you can hear. This third tone is called a binaural beat. You listen to it at the frequency difference between the two tones.

Binaural beats in the alpha frequencies (8 to 13Hz) encourage relaxation, promote positivity, and decrease anxiety.

Vs.

Binaural beats in the higher beta frequencies (14 to 30Hz) produce increased concentration and alertness, problem-solving, and improved memory.

Theta waves between 4 and 8Hz bring light sleep and deep relaxation. *Alpha waves* between 8 and 12Hz reflect the brain's idleness when you're not concentrating on anything.

Caffeine puts you into a Beta "focused" state, causing your body to produce cortisol, a stress hormone that gives you anxiety. That's why I stick to a lot of herbal tea while I focus and work set to the backdrop of music (even in writing this book). Giving it up helped me sleep better, renewed my sense of peace, and made me more emotionally even-keeled, tolerant with others, and patient in volatile business and life situations. I became more optimistic and saw the beauty around me. Many of us forget to appreciate it.

The standard 440Hz frequency to which all modern music is tuned turns off the brain's right hemisphere and creative areas. I'll spare you the Illuminati conspiracies about why that is, although I wrote a Citizen Kane-style manifesto/satire for SaaS, in case you'd like to read it.

While you do this process, you must focus on deep breathing as you would with meditation. Some people like to do this lying down or with their hands over their hearts, feeling their hearts beat. (hat tip Tony Robbins) Salvador Dali famously laid on a metal plate and held a key to ensure he didn't fall all the way to sleep. When he dozed off and dropped it, he'd hear the metallic clang and wake back up.

I work around the clock playing DNA repair, healing, and negative energy-reducing miracle tones. It decreases anxiety and helps me focus, but what's crazy is that it aligns with our optimal biorhythmic patterns, even down to the double helix structure of our DNA strands.

3. ACT AS IF:

You must live in your desired new identity 24/7. Test drive the Ferrari, tour the beautiful house, get on a yacht, network with dream clients, and live in that new reality of prosperity. "Act as if" the deal is already closed, and you're celebrating. Play it out mentally as having already happened, and be grateful for it. Reverse engineer it from closed-won. These real-life simulations put you into an "abundance feeling" to recall your vision in other exercises, harmonize with it, and shift it into your core identity.

Tony Robbins believes, "Change your state. Change your life." Your dream must manifest in reality once it's real in your mind. How and when will be determined by the depth of your belief, clarity of your vision, and certainty it's already come to pass. This concept is hidden because it's a paradox that violates our primitive understanding of the space-time continuum and how we've been taught the laws of the universe work. How can I be grateful for something that hasn't happened and is only a dream?

If God finished creating the entire multiverse, all variations of reality, past, present, and future, already exist in the quantum field. Like a painter with a blank canvas, your job is to choose the one you desire most at the moment *consciously*. This book aims to eliminate distortions you unknowingly create in your magnetic field so you can tune back into what you desire outside space and time. *Now*. And you can make it a game and have fun with this. Your desire to achieve any given goal indicates you can reach it. (Hat tip, Napoleon Hill)

"All that we see or seem is but a dream within a dream." – Edgar Allan Poe

4. DREAM BOARDS:

Let's say you want to close the perfect deal, possess a certain amount of money in your bank account, and reach an improved fitness level. You want to finally hit President's Club or get promoted to an account executive (AE), VP, or CRO. You want to earn one million dollars per year. Stare at these exact pictures you've cut out, put them on a poster board daily, and be grateful for them. You'll start reprogramming and shifting your subconscious mind into your real vision. *Becoming* is a dangerous word, forever pushing your desires out there on the horizon just out of reach. *Being* is *now.* Your mind does not know the difference between physical and imagined reality, and time is a manufactured construct.

You don't attract what you want. You attract what you are.

I call my Dream Board a "Reality Board" instead and build it digitally in Google Slides to pull it up and tap through it daily as a slideshow while listening to sacred music. I've got an old picture of my new books being #1 on Amazon, and it has already come true, thanks to you. I keep pictures of my accounts with new numbers in them.

In 1985, Jim Carrey wrote himself a ten million dollar check for "acting services rendered" dated Thanksgiving 1995. He kept it in his wallet to consistently remind him of his goal. Ten years later, just before Turkey Day, he got offered that exact amount for *Dumb and Dumber*. Legendary!

Have you ever sat down to think and write, "What is my ideal lifestyle, job, partner, investment, health and wealth level, quality of life, and mission?" You should!

I've used this process to attract the exact closed-won deal, income level, job, city, circumstance, relationship, etc. "My whole house is a dream board," shared my powerhouse friend Ari Rastegar, who is shaking up the real estate market in Austin. But what's odd is your dream often manifests in another, even better way if you're open to it. Just keep being grateful, know that all life is for you, and as I'll hammer into you: Remember, PRONOIA: the universe is plotting to do you good. Think of the world as your candy store and oyster, and boldly go after exactly what you want. Rather than chase after it, magnetize it to you.

Whether floating in a rooftop pool in Dubai or taking in the most incredible sunset in Venice, peak experiences I could have only dreamed of 20 years ago all came true. Even better. I had to let them in. I love this one:

> *"The 'hows' are the domain of the universe. It always knows the shortest, quickest, fastest, most harmonious way between you and your dream." – Mike Dooley*

5. JOURNALING:

Daily, I write down many goals as if they've already occurred in my present state of reality. I make I AM statements out of gratitude, like: "I am grateful I am helping thousands of people vastly improve their income."

"I'm ecstatic to see my business growing." "I am a magnet for money." Ultimately, you'll have one document you can carry with you, read, and re-read. And read again until it's your living document. Shout out to Peter McCammon, Ankush Jain, and Steve Hardison.

6. GRATITUDE:

Feeling grateful for things yet to happen to you is the highest level of summoning the law of attraction and manifestation. You are vibrating at the highest possible frequency. You are giving to others. Wanting others to have what you want most will pull things in even faster. The classic LOA formula is ASK, Believe, Receive, but I've come to think of it as...

I) *Know that you are worthy* of everything in God's creation, endowed with unique elements of genius singular to you.

II) **Be grateful for the future *in the now*** as if it's already occurred, and form a vivid mental picture of yourself in those moments as detailed as possible.

III) *Repeat this process as music* meets meditation meets visualization meets affirmation in a mash-up 2X per day, especially before sleep, to create an auto-suggestion in your subconscious.

IV) *Act!* When you wake up, trust your gut to take the actions necessary to get there. Look for signs and synchronicity. God will speak to you. Listen to the voice within.

7. LUCID DREAMING:

Have you ever had an out-of-body experience? Have you hovered above your bed or house looking down in a dream? Some people can astrally project their bodies into different dimensions. That's outside the scope of this book. Or, they take journeys with medicinal plants, unlocking their dormant pineal gland in the brain.

While I may not be ready to drop ayahuasca or DMT, focusing on my dreams before I sleep and repeating affirmations in my head will often influence my dreams, or I'll even go into a vivid dream state before bed. Deep Alpha/Theta states are always positive because they impact the psyche and reprogram negative or self-limiting beliefs. You're radiating at the frequency of pure love. When you're in the interspaces of conscious and unconscious awareness, only love is accessible to you, which is another indicator of the grand design of this universe. It's impossible to use the law of attraction to wish ill for others.

8. FEAR & DISCOMFORT:

If you're reading this cynically, you probably won't change. But some of you are finally ready. You want it so bad you can taste it, as much as breathing: life itself. But some of you are probably looking for some secret trick or something JM figured out that you haven't heard of. Here's your reminder that there is no "easy button." You must take 10X massive action toward your impossible goals and get uncomfortable.

"Hard choices, easy life. Easy choices, hard life."
– Jerzy Gregorek

Everything you want in life is on the other side of fear. Shocking your system with ice baths or going up high when you're afraid of heights will get you out of your comfort zone and teach your mind that a new identity is coming. One reason I love hot air balloon rides. You will harmonize with this new feeling just past your comfort zone. Cold call C-Levels and do two things that scare you before lunch, like my wealthy, self-made grandfather Joe always said was the secret to his success. [RIP]

I hated roller coasters and finally rode the highest wooden coaster on the border of Las Vegas on a dare. It shocks your ego and survival instinct in the juxtaposition of constantly seeking "safety" and comfort. Coaching and personal training work because they force you out of your comfort zone by shifting your being repeatedly until you cement that change into a new identity.

9. HYPNOSIS/NLP:

Believe it or not, we are only conscious of using 5% of our total brain capacity, and the subconscious powers 95% of our lives, so we consistently hypnotize ourselves with negative beliefs based on how chronically we think them. We are so hard on ourselves and constantly marinate on negative experiences in the past.

Flip this around through *Musifestation* and zoom in on the highlights of your life. You could think of this as positive brainwashing! Play your victories repeatedly in your head like a sports highlight reel. Only relive the good experiences; feel the joy, triumph, and delight. Then, build future experiences in your mind's eye as if they're happening now. While this isn't hypnosis, when you have run your mind through it so often that you're sure it's real, it *is*. That's the paradox.

While Tony Robbins gets much credit for neuro-linguistic programming (NLP) techniques and has excellent processes in his books (I remember doing *Personal Power* in the 90s with note cards), make sure to read the work of Richard

Bandler and John Grinder. Daniel Goleman's *Emotional Intelligence* and *Thinking, Fast and Slow* by Daniel Kahneman are also superb resources for understanding the inner workings of the mind. José Silva's *Mind Control Method* from 1977 has made a massive comeback. I had never heard of it when crafting *Musifestation*, but you'll find some overlaps that speak to the universal nature of these self-evident truths. The thing I haven't seen talked about is applying these principles to sales per se.

10. ***10X is the new 2X,*** the Benjamin Hardy and Dan Sullivan idea of 10Xing any goal. Cardone's Google Moonshot style rapidly eliminates pathways you can't take: the more impossible the goal, the fewer plausible routes. I would like to push it even farther to 100X, so it's nearly impossible in your current reality. Dream it as if it's already happening. Then, your brain, a supercomputer powered by the subconscious, will infinitely seek to manifest reality beyond your capacity. It goes back to putting your reticular activating system (RAS) to work on an insane problem to solve, but the brain is so powerful it can.

You will endlessly find new pathways to this goal—the idea of "divine right order" or synchronicity emerges. I talked about this in earlier methods.

Conversely, if you only create your future from what you physically see, it will always be limited.

The UNIVERSE is, in essence, plotting to do you good. That's the pronoia concept in action—the opposite of paranoia. When you outpour positive energy in one direction, positive things boomerang back in from another. That's why John Lennon sang, "Life is what happens when you're busy making other plans." Relationship karma!

Radiate positive vibrations and attract great things when you least expect it. When you fire up a prospecting campaign and boldly start developing business, putting out courage and positivity, eating rejection for breakfast, many times another deal comes flying in through the side window like a falcon when you'd least expect. It's like opening up a blocked flow of electromagnetic energy. A surge of power from within will pull things back into you, radiating at a similar frequency.

The law of attraction doesn't work because people just sit in a room dreaming, looking at vision boards, and never take necessary actions. What creates power? *Magnetism.* We are moving from a negative to a positive charge.

The great Greek philosopher Archimedes once said, "Give me a lever long enough and a fulcrum on which to place it, and I shall move the world."

Leverage. A lever can move your life forward exponentially with less effort, strain, and struggle. You need to consider the highest leveraged activities, and in sales, that's often calling in high at the C-Level.

The other issue is that you believe our human concept of time is accurate. We put the future far away and forget to create our "future from the future" in the now. (Werner Erhard) When you give all your faith, visualization, and gratitude to future events as being real now, you pull that parallel universe toward you.

You are a magnet, magnetizing and pulling that reality closer like a tractor beam. Raise your frequency and vibration, and other beings and circumstances vibrating at this level harmonize with you and pull in toward you. On a quantum physics level, you spawn infinite new universes instantly. Everything is energy: like attracts like.

> *"If you change the way you look at things, the things you look at change." – Wayne Dyer*

"I will be one day" is a cementing of forever "one day." Goal setting for 2025 pushes your goals out beyond 2030. You must live in the beautiful house *now* in your mind, smash your quota, drive your dream car, take the P-Club trip to Bali, achieve perfect health, be married to the perfect partner, achieve your desired income level, and build the ideal company––*now*.

You must assume the feeling of the wishes fulfilled. You must own, live, and make *I AM* statements from it. You must believe it with all your heart and soul and reprogram your subconscious mind with affirmations, visualizations, meditation, and music.

There are infinite parallel universes that always coexist, so you simply tune into or teleport to a new one with your new beliefs. From a neuroscience perspective, "You're installing new circuits in the brain that become hardwired. If you don't have the circuits in place, you'll default back to the old programs." (Dispenza)

How you feel shows you what you will manifest.

I remember the strangest riddle in Neville Goddard's book *The Power of Awareness*: "God hid the Godhead in the head of man." We are all creators and can summon new realities in no time. Rhonda Byrne taught us that "the hows are the domain of the universe, and the universe likes speed." Steve Jobs reaffirmed, "You can't connect the dots looking forward; you can only connect them looking backwards."

Quantum physicists have studied the ripple effect or butterfly effect. You can influence matter on the other side of the world just by thinking of it. Aka, "quantum entanglement." It's why a person in Japan can, through extra-sensory perception (ESP), read the mind of a loved one or sense a bad incident happening across oceans in California: again, the illusion of time and space. It also explains the phenomenon of "psychics." We are all connected infinitely, energetically, and everywhere to the one divine source. Einstein proved time is *relative*.

When procrastinating, we build up potential energy stored in our bodies via inertia, waiting for each subsequent kinetic burst. We inherently know what we should do to succeed in sales. In working with 1,000+ people, the block usually comes down to putting off prospecting. So follow *JMM 1.0* and *2.0* for the blueprint on what to do daily as an operating system for outbound sales.

No one is coming to save you, and when you realize that, it's the secret to taking full responsibility and creating lasting change in your life. Learn to rely on yourself and maintain a healthy respect for yourself and your innate abilities. You *can* own your own destiny. Focus on daily RGAs - revenue-generating activities. (hat tip, Ian Koniak)

Take proactive ACTIONS like:

- List building (laser-targeting dream 100 clients or look-a-likes á la Chet Holmes)
- Making cold calls to humans you know can buy (3% in the buying window)
- Initiating chat flows on LinkedIn with the Fourth Frame (see *JMM 1.0*)
- Doing 30 to 50 triples per day: "call, voicemail, email" under 90 seconds flat (*Combo Prospecting*)
- Taking the 900 Challenge (contact 30 strangers per day for one month – but don't stop there!)

- Relentlessly following up on active opportunities and fearlessly digging up the ones that ghosted you

Now imagine DOING all this from a radically shifted new place of being. Imagine executing with champion thoughts, positive self-talk, and unshakeable belief. You will be, in a word, unstoppable—a life-enhancing force of nature. Unleash your inner rainmaker.

> *"Praxis is the integration of belief with behavior. You will never accomplish anything until you believe you can." – Bob Proctor*

It works the same as with fitness: the heaviest weight you'll ever lift is the door to the gym. Anyone can see that the above activities will yield pipeline and thus revenue. So what's holding you back? Your mindset. Your fear of failure. And the real kicker that impacts many of my high-achieving clients is *fear of success*. Can you imagine?

It's chronic. I'll ask, "What is this bringing up for you?" And they'll remember their parent saying, "Money is the root of all evil." Or, "If you get rich, you'll never see your family." Just processing what the negative tie is to your hidden past often unblocks you so you can create the life you want. Awareness moves us from value conflict to value alignment.

Eliminating self-imposed mental obstacles stemming from deceptively simple (or traumatic) childhood experiences can create a breakthrough. We're programmed very young to believe limitations about ourselves that we may never question. Remember the baby elephant metaphor; now giant, tied by the tiniest chain, it could snap, but it doesn't even try. That's you; that's all of us in some respects.

When you shift your identity to that of a top sales performer, your values and vision are now aligned, and you'll be extremely frustrated if you don't take massive action. You'll raise your standards naturally. Every human intrinsically knows what they need to do to be happy, but typically is self-sabotaging: blocking themselves.

Abundance and prosperity are our birthright: native, healthy states. We are not our story. We must exorcise our demons and move from a victim to an owner to realize our ultimate destiny. (Chandler)

Find a big enough *why*, and the *how* will show up.

Many of you convince yourselves that you are blocked from getting what you truly want in this life, and you may want to toss this book out in frustration, feeling like you've heard it all before. I get it; I've been there. It can be very depressing, blathering on about happiness. ;-)

But there's a deeper reason *why you're stuck*. And so I'll close this chapter with inspiration from Bob Proctor's exceptional work on shifting your inner paradigm to unblock manifestation and immediately make the law of attraction work for you.

"A Paradigm is a multitude of habits fixed in our subconscious mind that we act on without any conscious thought. And it's our actions that produce our Results.

THERE ARE TWO KNOWN WAYS TO CHANGE A PARADIGM:

1. CONSTANT SPACED REPETITION OF IDEAS THAT ARE ESSENTIALLY OPPOSITE THE PARADIGM

2. PERSONAL EXPERIENCE OF AN EMOTIONAL IMPACT

Change your paradigms, and you will change the way you create results."

I understand that it can sometimes be challenging to feel positive and hopeful about the future. However, I want you to know that this once radical, powerful concept can transform your life, and I am living proof. Breakthroughs in quantum physics continue to demystify it. I know that it might seem like a long journey, but I assure you that you won't have to wait as long as I did to experience the benefits of this "law." It can give you hope and a fresh perspective on life. I urge you to read the entire book and complete all the exercises for the next 90 days to see your results. I understand that it can be hard to stay motivated, but don't lose faith.

The *JMM Book Series* has been a game-changer for many readers, and I have seen incredible transformations. For instance, Srba Markovic read it repeatedly for two months (it sits on his desk), and his outbound team's results skyrocketed! Scott Martinis clarified his vision, pivoted his agency, and cold-started his client base to $30K per month within 30 days. As Alex Hormozi rightly said, "You gain more from reading one great book five times than reading five mediocre books. I'll read a book until I can teach it." So, don't give up; keep reading, learning, and growing. Remember, you are not alone; we can overcome any obstacle together.

> *"Whatever we plant in our subconscious mind and nourish with repetition and emotion will one day become a reality." – Earl Nightingale*

CHAPTER 2

Optimize results with *JMM*™

"No human is kept poor because opportunity has been taken away from them. Nature is an inexhaustible store-house of riches; the supply will never run short. Thought is the only power which can produce tangible riches . . . To think what you want to think is to think TRUTH, regardless of appearances."

– Wallace Wattles

My GM, Jim Mongillo, used to say this. You can't do a 7-figure deal if you don't picture it working out beforehand. We must anchor the sale and set the tone from the outset. "The swagger breeds," he added. But he was more like Columbo than the Wolf of Wall Street. He loved listening to people and is still the most personable human I know.

Charisma is an X-factor anyone can develop.

I'm often asked, "How can I grow my confidence like you have JM when I haven't been selling for 20 years?" Confidence = self-esteem. We talked about it in *JMM 1.0* and *2.0* - top 2 ways. Deal with your childhood trauma before the age of 7 in a Freudian/ Jungian modality via psychotherapy - it helps! Get humble, and get it done (ongoing).

Second way: my interpretation of David C. Baker's "market validation" principle: get "so good they can't ignore you," as Steve Martin prophetically said (great Cal Newport book). Develop expertise and drive excellent results. Then save every last recommendation, reference, and piece of positive feedback screenshotted in a file. Review it often. Share it with prospects. Let it build you up internally.

Thirdly? Love. It's the most powerful force in the universe, so "show 'em you know 'em" (McKenna/Toland) and that you care. Go out of your way to do some research and personalize your interactions. Curiosity is a form of love.

> *"There is no greater power in the Universe than the power of love. The feeling of love is the highest frequency you can emit. If you could wrap every thought in love, if you could love everything and everyone, your life would be transformed." – Rhonda Byrne*

The hidden one is: decide now. Even within a seemingly unconfident, low self-esteem person's private life, there are some areas where they confidently give 10X: with family, with friends, playing their favorite sports or video games, when they compete with their siblings. It's just in selling situations, it feels like skydiving. They get nervous, have clammy palms, break into a cold sweat, and suffer. People often fear public speaking more than jumping out of a plane.

I always tell clients, "I can't jump out of the plane for you. I can't dial CXOs for you. I can't get under the bar; flex your muscles and bench press the weight for you. *You* have to flex. You have to decide. If you have the will, I can teach you the skill."

And this one cracks me up, "I want to learn to skydive - every aspect, I just don't want to jump out of the plane. Can we skip that part?" See the metaphor. You must be willing to press outside your comfort zone and take on the hard things. The sting of failure and rejection means you're growing, so cultivate a growth mindset. Tremendous friction and pressure create a diamond, so welcome adversity. You get the privilege to triumph over it and cultivate grit.

That's why coaching works; fundamentally, this word means "encouragement." (hat tip, Steve Chandler) We often cannot see our own blind spots without a grizzled guide.

Now that we've gone into the fundamentals of all the ways to action on LOA, the law of attraction, let's bring this down to practical art and science.

Write down your sales goals in Evernote and read them to yourself daily from a mobile device. There's no megalomania here. Believe in your ability as a creator to generate results.

Creativity is a massive secret to standing out in sales communication. I recommend all my clients read *The Purple Cow* by Seth Godin. Most selling inhabits a stuffy realm of tradition and conformity. How will you be the signal in the noise when your outreach looks identical to everyone else's?

By now, you have mastered *JMM 1.0 & 2.0* (if not, read/reread them). Armed with every last prospecting strategy and tactic you could ever need to make revenue happen improvisationally with flair, you will prevail in all seasons. Let your freak flag fly, be your true self, and stand out as Seth Godin's "purple cow." Turn heads, be provocative with challenger insights, and your dream clients will take notice. Like the iconic jazz standard's refrain, "There will never be another you."

Example affirmations for sellers

(Make a list of 100 of these, and say them 2X per day):

> I AM UNSTOPPABLE
>
> I AM #1 IN MY COMPANY AND INDUSTRY
>
> I AM EARNING COMMISSION EFFORTLESSLY
>
> I AM WINNING PRESIDENT'S CLUB
>
> I AM DRIVING IMMENSE VALUE TO MY CUSTOMERS
>
> I AM EASILY CRUSHING MY QUOTA
>
> IT'S EFFORTLESS FOR ME TO OVERACHIEVE MY NUMBER
>
> I AM PHENOMENAL AT SELLING OUR PRODUCT
>
> EVERYTHING GOES RIGHT FOR ME IN THIS DEAL
>
> I AM TRIUMPHANTLY CLOSING 6 AND 7 FIGURES
>
> MONEY COMES TO ME EASILY AND FREQUENTLY
>
> I AM ALWAYS GETTING PROMOTED
>
> I LOVE MONEY AND MONEY LOVES ME
>
> I AM WORTHY OF... [SUCCESS, LOVE, PEACE, MY DREAM] (insert all the things you deserve)

This stuff may seem "woo woo" to you, but the more you orient your mind this way, the more you build a champion's mentality and positively wired spiritual DNA. For any of these methods to work and take root, you must love yourself so that you can compassionately love others. Be that trusted advisor who can truly serve everyone you come in contact with.

Kill your profit motive. Aim to serve. It's like a doctor taking the Hippocratic oath: "I will do no harm." (hat tip Alan Weiss) Prospects sense it—everything shifts. Read *The Go-Giver* by Bob Burg.

With a mind racing around 70,000 chaotic thoughts per day, the same as a billionaire, celebrity, or sports star's, you need to remember another mantra: You are not your thoughts, mind, or body; you are the consciousness – the "I am" – behind this mechanism of your mind. Your self-perception and self-image will dictate your ability to be successful in sales. Your exact salary. Your exact health, wealth, and happiness. Pass or fail.

Here's the trash in an average seller's head: "I'm not sure this deal will come in. I'm not confident about bringing up the money. What if I call a CEO and they find out I'm an imposter? Maybe I'm not good enough. I don't deserve to hit quota. I'm always failing. I don't think my manager likes me. This customer is so irritating and keeps ghosting me. I can't believe how unfair the comp plan is. This job is so stressful and hard."

We flip that in *JMM 3.0*: "I love my manager, I love my job, I love my customers, this product is selling like wildfire in the market. I can easily call CXOs and enjoy it. I can transform this prospect's business. I can *easily* do 7 figure deals. I'm worthy of going to P-Club. I'm fantastic at sales. I am unstoppable."

Imposter syndrome, which affects 70% of people, from interns to CROs per KPMG, can only happen if you listen to your negative thoughts that are primarily composed of subconscious lies. Stop listening. Reprogram your core.

Are self-limiting beliefs true? Logically, never.

If you need to gain new skills, get a coach. Read my Codex guides. If you're reading this, you can become a champion. There's absolutely nothing anyone can do that you can't! Your desire to break through means it's within you. It's a sign. The real you, your inner voice is whispering. Let it grow louder until it drowns out the Gollum living in your head.

Always add the feeling of gratitude for the things you wish to see that are already happening in your mind. It's efficient. "I'm so grateful this deal just came over the line right in time for Q4 close." Doing this, I was able to close a $600K, 2-year deal displacing five competitors. You'd be shocked at what's possible to manifest rapidly. Imagine your prospect calling five competitors to "break up" with them on the last day of Q4 because you orchestrated a better deal. True story!

Outwardly, you win when you outsell your competitors. But the real reason you win is when you outsell them *in your own mind.*

Our strategy and tactics for tech stack consolidation to lower TCO (total cost of ownership) were rock solid on the deal above. We'd built a robust business case and clear ROI. Still, our mindset of getting this done allowed us to move heaven and Earth toward us at the 11th hour. We never relinquished hope and stuck steadfast to our vision that it would close. On the last day of the year, 234 emails and 36 cold calls later, we sealed the deal with a former Coast Guard Lieutenant negotiating hard to prove a point to his team.

"Never, ever ever ever ever give up." – Winston Churchill

When I was 31, sitting in the Bay area and getting rejected left and right, I used the music meets meditation process at the heart of this book, which became the whitepaper *Musifestation.* I went from $45K to over $100K overnight, working directly for Sean Parker, the world's youngest billionaire who co-founded Facebook.

My dream manifested for me because my investors in my late 20s incubator days made an introduction to one of the co-founders. Because I had a great niche specialization in closing nonprofit fundraising SaaS deals, I was more of an expert than the other candidates applying for the role. I refused to take no for an answer and leveraged the heck out of my network despite a perceived lack of qualifications and experience. I got a foot in the door and spent years after that lucky break developing deep SaaS sales experience (and selling into Enterprise) starting from zero.

> *"You have to create your own luck. You have to be aware of the opportunities around you and take advantage of them." – Bruce Lee*

But I hadn't even seen the opportunity or category of activism and fundraising SaaS coming. I was applying for SEO roles and traditional social media and MarTech stuff like LinkedIn and Salesforce and getting shut down left and right due to lack of degree automatically spit out by the vetting algorithm. Very soon, I'd ride the wave of the mobile revolution.

Remember the comfort zone? I was willing to move anywhere in the world to move up in tech. I envisioned myself accomplishing my goals so vividly and took action relentlessly, applying myself to master selling wherever I went. Within two years of using *Musifestation*, I landed the Salesforce role. Within five years, I worked for LinkedIn in the Empire State Building. My journey starts (and finishes) in LA and then moves to Palo Alto, St. Louis, NYC, and Seattle. Now, I'm always traveling the world and helping clients on every continent crack the top funnel.

That's why my coaching methodology is so deep and creates radical transformation.

1. We pinpoint and shatter your limiting beliefs around yourself, money, and success: how do you sabotage and hold yourself back? What are the lies you tell yourself? Your money fears? How do *you* block you? If you don't have a coach to help you with this, inspect your thoughts and question if they're true á la Eckhart Tolle, Syd Banks & Byron Katie.

2. We finally figure out your unique genius and God-given aptitude that you're overlooking, which you can develop by turning up the dial to 11, productizing, monetizing, and scaling it up as a primary or side hustle.

3. We create shortcuts based on our collective experience. 1+1 = 11. My 20+ years multiplied by your many years of experience equals an instant quantum leap. Let's set a 100X impossible goal and find new vectors from A-Z, jumping through the wormhole of the space-time continuum into 4th-dimensional reality.

Time is an illusion. The universe likes speed. Once you stop mentally shackling yourself to your past and limiting beliefs, your supercomputer brain can take over and catapult you into infinite arrays of new universes—the ones you'd like to see *if* you program your subconscious correctly.

Syd Banks illuminated the *3 Principles* paradigm of Mind, Consciousness, and Thought as the fundamental parameters of our existence. Michael Neill wrote, "We are living in the feeling of our thinking."

After reading this book, the only regret you'll ever have is not "thinking big enough." You need to dream bigger. The solution to every problem is to "think bigger," not play small: play full out.

Jeff Bezos truly encapsulates the spirit of thinking big in Amazon's core leadership principles. "Think big. Thinking small is a self-fulfilling prophecy. Leaders create and communicate a bold direction that inspires results. They think differently and look around corners for ways to serve customers." (hat tip Aaron Norris, rockstar client and coach, former AWS)

JMM™ is like a superpower. I went from account management to a beast at outbound sales, developing my methods from the first principles of logic and neuroscience. David Sandler, Mike Bosworth, and Aaron Ross inspired me to develop a distinct voice of my own, especially around cracking top-of-funnel and emergent AI-powered sales automation.

> *"If I have seen further, it is by standing on the shoulders of Giants." – Sir Isaac Newton, 1675*

SNAP Selling by Jill Konrath was the first book I ever read on sales after ten years of thinking I was a "natural" and never making a move to better myself. Talk about fixed mindset arrogance. By the time I'd honed in on the *Justin Michael Method* (*JMM*™) tactical elements in my other books, I was doing six years of pipeline in 6 months. I remember grinding alone on the phones in a cold back room in Chinatown, taking the subway train to Little Italy, and walking through a blizzard alone with my thoughts. In those days, I was developing a new omnichannel blended combination selling method, which became the basis for *Combo Prospecting.*

"If you set yourself on fire, the world will come and watch you burn," I thought, channeling my inner John Wesley. I'd done many charity events and concert promotions back in my day, so this was another mantra in my head. I was just finding the discipline to make the most calls in mobile marketing, a niche sector where everybody networked over cocktail parties and relied on warm intros or inbound, some doing basic mail merges. Sequencing wasn't even really happening at this time. We had Groove (now Clari) and were ahead of the game.

> *"Where you place your attention is where you place your energy. Once you fix your attention or your awareness or your mind on possibility, you place your energy there as well. As a result, you're affecting matter with your attention or observation. The placebo effect is not fantasy, then; it's quantum reality. Energy." – Dr. Joe Dispenza*

When I think of why *JMM*™ is so pivotal, it's another mindset shift: you focus. When you shift your curiosity, you listen in a new way. By creating a "you" focus or other orientation on the customer, your calls go longer, prospects trust you faster, open up, and share their true pain. You create the desire within the prospect. Garrett MacDonald instilled this Jeffrey Gitomer nugget into me, "People love to buy but hate to be sold." The polarity must shift. Now, you can get to the bottom of what's really been troubling them. Now, you can genuinely serve them.

> *"The best way to find yourself is to lose yourself in the service of others." – Mahatma Gandhi*

There are a bunch of visualization exercises that I use daily. But the main ones look like this. Create a REALITY BOARD, distinct from the traditional "vision board," based on the erroneous title, which implies you *will* or *muscle* circumstances into being. We will discuss willpower and how "effortlessness" is "the way." But you create a file with pictures of everything you want in your life, and I mean precisely. You should also write that list down with grateful "I AM" statements as close as possible to how you see it.

I AM EARNING $500K PER YEAR

I AM ECSTATIC TO OWN MY DREAM HOME

I AM THE CRO OF [FAVORITE SAAS COMPANY]

I AM EASILY PAYING OFF MY DEBT

I AM A LINKEDIN TOP VOICE

I AM TRANSFORMING LIVES

I AM BLESSED BY GOOD LUCK

Try this one on for size: one of my favorite affirmations I still use to this day.

"God is my infinite supply, and large sums of money come to me quickly and easily under the grace of God for the greater good of all concerned. I am happily and easily earning, saving, and investing over one million dollars annually." – Jack Canfield

What gets in your way? Your ego craves fear.

"Part X is an invisible force that keeps you from changing." The unassuming celebrity psychiatrist Phil Stutz wisely explains how our darkness and shadow self hold us back in the stellar Netflix documentary by Jonah Hill entitled *Stutz*. Identifying our shadow self and radically *accepting it* is paramount to happiness. As Rhonda says, "nothing negative can remain in the face of love." We all have a dark side to embrace or run from. I love Phil's "tools" (check out the book by the same name) for getting our minds right, and thanks to my friend Joseph Miller for turning me on to them.

"Only when we are brave enough to explore the darkness will we discover the infinite power of our light." – Brené Brown

Back to F.E.A.R. It stands for future events appearing real. I searched for the origins of this acronym, and it goes back even further to Mark Twain:

"Do you worry unnecessarily about the future? Remember, most fears are just False Evidence Appearing Real. Don't let unfounded fears rob you of the joys of life, or you, too, will say, there has been much tragedy in my life, and at least half of it actually happened."

The opposite of fear of your future is realizing that positive events can *be real* now. It all comes down to what you believe and chronically think in your mind. Your brain cannot tell the difference between a vivid dream and reality. Hook up an MRI, and the brain fires electrical signals the same way in both cases. So what will you choose? Be happy now. Decide what is real in the now, in real-time, and shift your being, reprogramming your subconscious mind and shifting your self-image.

I'm hammering this concept home repeatedly in this book because it's the only road to freedom. It's the polar opposite of what we are taught in modern society. You won't find it in a shot of Botox or at the bottom of a glass. We chase money, status, beauty, pleasure, and instant gratification when everything we're looking for is already within us, God-given from birth.

Slow down to speed up. To scale, do the unscalable.

Let's visualize together the world we'd like to see, the role we'd like to play, our highest self. Who are you being? What is your impact? Your legacy? Have you thought about it lately? As you visualize, meditate, affirm, and state your triumphal I AM phrases.

Meditate to sacred geometric music; your mind will rear up and fight you like a demon. "You're not good enough; you'll never have that. You can't succeed." I call these value conflicts. But your heart is a compass that always knows the way to true North, even if your head tries to trick you.

Gandhi meant this when he said, "Be the change that you wish to see in the world." It's the nature of this fractal holographic universe. "As above so below, as within so without." The Emerald Tablet decoded. We know three dimensions exist, but there are likely many higher ones outside the visible light spectrum. Many schools of thought believe our brains can tap into them, harkening back to a distant time of myth like Plato's Atlantis and Lemuria.

Lift yourself to great heights of joy, peace, and serenity, and unlock inner seeing. Decide now to be positive in this moment. In every moment, you always have a *conscious* choice.

> *"The purpose of life is joy! When you're in joy, you attract the highest and best in every area of your life. Joy increases to the exact degree that you deliberately increase your good thoughts, good words, and good actions. I've found in my life that the easiest way to increase my joy is to religiously practice gratitude until I'm a gratitude machine!"*
> *– Rhonda Byrne*

What if, before a big meeting, you proactively visualize the best-case scenario instead of worrying, letting negative self-talk flow in, and imagining the worst-case scenario automatically?

Olympic athletes walk through their sprint in their minds before the run. F1 race car drivers run through all the turns of a specific track in their heads, planning how they'll brake, accelerate, and out-maneuver their opponents before a big race.

A client confessed, "I'm not doing the 4th frame or initiating new business chat flows with prospects because if I succeed, I'll be unhappy." I questioned where that came from. His father had warned him that if you really "make a lot of money, you'll never see your family." This memory paralyzed his ability to do the outbound prospecting necessary to create his call coaching business effectively.

I coached him to realize the truth is the inverse: abundance and prosperity would allow him to help his family and church more. And that it would be even more stressful to stay at the income level he was at, caught up in a business he didn't have as much passion for.

Once he pinpointed the self-sabotage of his thoughts, the breakthrough came swiftly - the procrastination stopped, and he built positive inertia. He booked 10 Zoom calls that day, leveraging the 4th frame (see *Sales Superpowers: JMM*™ *1.0* for the complete method).

I'm a big fan of a book called *Zero Limits* by Joe Vitale, also in *The Secret*. He introduces a process called Ho'oponopono, a healing and cleansing ritual from Hawaiian mysticism. This book perfectly coincides with what we're talking about in shifting ourselves to the level of our primary identity and its downstream impact on others.

The core of Alcoholics Anonymous is to let go of resentment. Resentments are the mind-killer. Rhonda Byrne reveals, "If you are full of resentment, what you will attract is more people, circumstances, and events that will cause resentment."

In Ho'oponopono, you repeat this phrase and mean it with all your heart: "I'm sorry, I love you, please forgive me, thank you." The book recounts the story of how psychologist Ihaleakala Hew Len cured criminally insane patients just by reading their charts and repeating this process. And he never even met them!

Now mix Ho'oponopono with the power of *Musifestation*. Sit comfortably, maybe cross your legs, close your eyes, put on music at 432Hz that relaxes your brain into an Alpha, Theta state, and visualize what you want by repeating: "I'm sorry, I love you, please forgive me, thank you." The order of the phrases does not matter.

Do you want to take this to the next level? Think of people who have wronged you, hurt you, whom you resent, and bless them with those words and thoughts of true forgiveness. Do this "cleaning" until all your thoughts are clear and you feel only LOVE. Pray for people you don't like. Instead of hate, choose love.

You are the lotus blossom unfolding under the moonlight of peace.

Want good things for them and bless them. I know it's hard, but WWJD: what would Jesus do, or Buddha or the Dalai Lama? We *practice* compassion to create a brighter world. We aim to achieve Christ Consciousness: divine love, spiritual integration, and heart awakening.

We will discuss brain wave functional states below your normal, caffeinated Beta focus. However, it is vital to understand Gamma's purpose, the state above Beta (oscillating far faster at 35Hz and above). This wave is associated with problem-solving and concentration.

According to Joe Dispenza, you can access this state differently by focusing your attention on your heart. All the brain frequencies align from the lowest to the highest, reaching up toward Gamma (above Beta), allowing you to radiate high-frequency manifestation energy, transmuting the physical universe toward your highest inner vision and tapping into your dormant *supernatural* abilities. He describes this *flow* state as "ecstasy, connection to something greater: bliss."

Essentially, your brain becomes a tuning fork in the quantum field. Like attracts like, so you attract what you put out. Joy attracts joy. I can't help but think of the immortal Louis Armstrong lyric, "When you're smiling, the whole world smiles with you." I love how Rhonda eloquently puts it in recent interviews reflecting on decades of practicing the secret (since our chance meetings), "When you're in *joy*, you'll manifest so fast. It's a really high frequency, and you'll manifest quickly. If you're in grief or despair, it's very slow because that's a protective mechanism."

Nirvana comes from the Sanskrit words "nis" (out) + "vā" (blow): to blow out or extinguish. It's fascinating how the full definition in Oxford Languages ties everything we've been discussing together: *"a transcendent state in which there is neither suffering, desire, nor sense of self, and the subject is released from the effects of karma and the cycle of death and rebirth."*

Let go of all the negativity in your body, mind, heart, and soul. To me, this is the essence of prayer. And this is unlocking the sheer power of the secret. Miracles can now enter your life from a pure mind, clean heart, and soul. From the formless infinite nature of a higher power flowing through you like water carving rock, you're leveraging the cosmic rudder or "lathe of God."

I always describe it this way: inspired by *The Lathe of Heaven* (1971), a superb science fiction novel by Ursula K. Le Guin, nominated for the Hugo and Nebula awards, where the main character's dreams could alter past and present reality. Not too far off from the truth! A lathe is a machine tool that shapes wood or metal, much like the power of your mind to shape your reality.

Behold the infinite power of your subconscious to impact the ONE mind that is *all* and thereby touches all others.

We are all interconnected as the universe is fractal holographic, so our positive thoughts and prayers for others can shift their being and minds; the theory would have it. For simplicity, a fractal is a mathematical pattern that, when zoomed in on, infinitely repeats, like zooming in on the coastline of Brazil. Holograms are the same in one part as in every part.

These are useful metaphors for the UNITY of the human spirit with all flora and fauna on this electromagnetic Earth machine that Nikola Tesla described as a giant "Tesla coil." Don't even get me started on toroidal, aetheric, or telluric *free* energy sources from the Earth and sky; that's the subject of another book, and many believe why Tesla's tower got shut down by the oil, steel, and railroad magnates.

The implications are staggering: our thoughts create our own world, can influence others, and even create the world as a whole. Hence, what astounded me about the Hawaiian psychologist healing his patients remotely with Ho'oponopono was that even the plants and trees around him started to grow back and get healthier.

We are all composed of star matter made of energy down to its very essence. Radiating positive energy creates a ripple effect on all living things around you. If you want to go down a rabbit hole, look into "remote viewing," historical mapmaking, and paranormal activities where observers access the inner mind to do what's considered impossible by modern science.

When we study all the ascended masters on Earth, from Buddha to Jesus to the Dalai Lama, we see the harmonization of positive energy, compassion, and love creating a change in the physical universe. A change in your mental and spiritual vibration shifts your magnetic field. From walking on water to parting the Red Sea to all manner of miracles, the holy grail of life is in harnessing your energy to that of pure love; never fear.

There is only fear or love, and the vast majority of people live a *fear-based* life of slow suffocation and silent torture. While fear is addictive, love can be just as addictive.

So try this out. Find someone you hate, despise, and resent, and pray for them. Forgive them, let go of your resentments, and repeat this: "I'm sorry, please forgive me, thank you, I love you."

> *"Everything that's coming into your life, you are attracting into your life. And it's attracted to you by virtue of the images you're holding in your mind. It's what you're thinking. Whatever is going on in your mind you are attracting to you!"* – Bob Proctor

We are 100% responsible for our own lives. Denial is Egypt's longest river. As Jack Canfield, my first mentor, preaches, that is the *first* success principle. The truth will set you free. The lie is that it's anyone else's fault.

If you seek a breakthrough in your life, be grateful for it, as if it's already happened every night before you sleep. When you wake up, the universe will have changed. Explore the complete works of Neville Goddard.

I read all his work, and there are wild stories where a soldier had to return to his family and dreamed of being honorably discharged every night for months and then suddenly was. In another case, an entrepreneur visualized his last name on a sign in the city on a big building every day for a year, and suddenly, circumstances aligned, so his store was acquired. Ultimately, his name appeared on the sign.

Imagine checks showing up at random in the mail. Imagine job offers flowing in. Imagine inbound inquiries out of the clear blue. Imagine deals closing effortlessly and seeing the mutually executed DocuSign agreement come through. Take it one step further: *expect* it. *Assumption* sets the law of attraction into action.

> *"Remember this: anticipation is the ultimate power. Losers react; leaders anticipate." – Tony Robbins*

Here is an unstoppable process to attract anything you want, synergizing all the available ideas.

1. Visualize down to the finest grain detail what you want in life, paint a mental picture of it, and put it on your dream board, "reality board, remember!" Write it down in the most explicit description possible. You often weren't specific enough when it didn't manifest or manifested wrongly. You forgot to incorporate *giving*.

2. State out loud how you ARE it, how you are grateful for it, and see it in your mind as having already happened. Remember, we don't attract what we want. We attract what we *are*. Now flip it and want it for someone else more than yourself. Move from take to GIVE to avoid the curse of greed.

3. Relive the imagery as you enter an Alpha or Theta state between consciousness and unconsciousness with music. Watch the negative self-talk come up for you and question each negative thought á la Syd Banks, Byron Katie, and

Eckhart Tolle. Ask yourself, "Is it true?" as Byron Katie does in *The Work*.

All your stress will not serve you. It's mainly self-created; let go of it.

> *"If I can teach you anything, it is to identify the stressful thoughts that you're believing and to question them, to get still enough so that you can hear your own answers. Stress is a gift that alerts you to your asleepness. Feelings like anger or sadness exist only to alert you to the fact that you're believing in your own stories." – Byron Katie*

Of course, you are worthy. Of course, you are good enough. You are a child of God and have no reason to play small. We exist to make manifest the glory of God. Marianne Williamson had it right in *Return to Love*, reflecting on *A Course in Miracles*.

The law of attraction breaks down for sellers because they create a "special hour of prayer" and sporadically picture their goals and dreams. They think of the future as "out there." You need to pull your future into your present or "create your future from your future," my interpretation of Werner Erhard's quote meets LOA.

Now, we see the prophecy of "10X as the new 2X" thinking. Dan Sullivan and Dr. Benjamin Hardy talk about this, but I'll tell you what it means to me and my experience.

Trust your inner knowing, your inner seeing, and your inner vision. Form a healthy self-perception of who you are as an infinite spiritual being.

Unleash yourself from the chains of self-doubt. BE what you wish to receive. The genie in Aladdin's lamp is *you* harmonizing with a higher power (the universe). But to make things happen in your life, you must take action. A massive step is the power of ASKING. (Read *The Aladdin Factor*, Canfield/Victor Hansen). All selling is an endless series of BOLD asks and harsh rejections. Go for the "no." (Richard Fenton)

> *"If the whole world rejected you and you didn't believe any of your thoughts about it, you'd be completely at peace." – Byron Katie*

When you feel the sting of getting shut down, practice compassion: do not judge the prospect. That would be hypocritical because think about how many sellers you've shut down in your life: that's just karma.

You must take action. Find that inner wisdom and gut instinct. Your inner voice will lead you to where you should go. Like *The Alchemist* by Paulo Coelho, where the protagonist goes on a journey of discovery to exotic far-off lands only to find the treasure he sought was right there at his feet the whole time where he began, your journey of self-discovery begins and ends with Marcel Proust's "seeing the existing world with new eyes."

The treasure you seek is sitting under your chair. Right between your ears. In your heart. The power of God you seek is within you, connected to everything else: all matter, space, energy, and time. You can access this in a literal instant and then take the next best action on it.

Synchronicity and signs are the universe speaking to you. As you align with your vision, you're grateful for it in advance. You're *acting as if* it's already happening. You will start to see signs and alignment everywhere. That's the miraculous and mystical piece of living this stuff for nearly two decades.

The original idea for this book was *action and attraction* because that's the component most "law of attraction" resources miss. When I stumbled upon these principles, I rewrote my resume from the strongest frame I could muster, a vantage point of power. One recruiter in SF told me, "You look larger than life here. Tamp it down. There's no way you can send this out."

Then, I landed the gig for Sean Parker. Then, I worked for Salesforce. Then, LinkedIn. I acquired complete confidence in my ability by taking stock of my accomplishments over the course of my life. Rather than base my self-esteem on a diploma, badge, or certificate, I simply remember my triumphs. I extrapolated what was possible for my new employer based on those inalienable traits.

Bold action and the secret follow the compass of fear and discomfort:

1. Calling C-levels
2. Going after jobs way above your pay grade
3. Targeting Chet Holmes's "Dream 100" companies that are the best fits for your ICP vs. avoiding them, thinking you're not ready
4. Moving to another city to change your environment and networking within a new community. Jim Rohn reminds us, "We are the average of our five closest people."
5. Quitting habitual negative thinking, giving up drinking, starting to exercise, stopping your judgments and trash-talking or gossiping about other people, seeking to admire rather than tear them down, stopping all the people pleasing and approval-seeking. Why follow when you can lead?

Why even endeavor to earn one million dollars a year or more? I recently put up a poll asking, "Would you rather make one million dollars per year stressfully or earn $250K per year without stress?" Remarkably, on 250 votes, it was a perfectly even split. But my friend Mark America Smith wrote a wise retort:

> *"Anyone who chooses $250K without stress instead of $1,000,000 with stress is either already wealthy or totally out of their mind.*
>
> *Five years of stress and $5,000,000 in earnings is something less than 0.01% of humans will ever have the chance to earn. It is life-changing and worth the stress.*
>
> *Invested properly, it is also worth 40 years of $250,000 per year stress-free income."*

If I hadn't fallen into sales in 2001, I'd never have become a sales manager. If I hadn't met Patrick and became a marketing director and inside seller in incubators in 2006, I would never have met the investors who introduced me to Joe Green and Sean Parker. If I'd never believed I could go to Salesforce, I never would have *attracted* a way to get there by helping my first VP of Sales, JT, land a great gig in the Valley.

Suppose I'd never have found Tony J. Hughes as my mentor in Sydney by typing in "challenge to Challenger" on YouTube and brazenly reaching out to Tony for mentorship once I read *The Joshua Principle*. In that case, I'd never have read 200+ sales books, created my methodology, gotten to apply my knowledge in the VC-backed world, gone on to be a top VP of Sales in SaaS, written multiple bestselling books, and launched a 7-figure consultancy, helping thousands of people and companies.

Looking back, it's all interconnected and logical, but I was navigating a path of blind faith. "Fate is what we make." Did I just inadvertently quote John Connor in *Terminator 2*? ;-)

I couldn't see the whole staircase. I just took the next step, á la MLK. As fog lights into a deep fog, I could only see 10 meters ahead as I navigated. I love that Jack concept. A plane course corrects consistently the whole time it flies. Shifting being is that spiritual course correction. A great coach can hold you accountable to that shift and locate the blind spots outside your radar screen. It's like in *The Last Crusade*, where Indiana Jones steps off the ledge, and the bridge suddenly appears. "The penitent man shall pass," Sean Connery mutters under his breath as he lies dying before drinking water from the grail saves him.

I vividly recall sitting in my backyard back in 2020 and watching the breeze softly move through the leaves of a Japanese cherry tree. I contemplated going off on my own and cutting the cord on working for corporations, and I saw the vision of burning the boats.

Would I work for myself, making millions quickly, or continue to make tens of millions for others, slowly seeing a sliver of my output? Instantly, I visualized building up a sustainable, successful consulting practice. Then, I did it, and the rest, as they say, is history.

Musifestation Core Exercise:

1. *Listen to specially tuned sacred music (432/528Hz)*

2. *Breathe deep from your stomach until you relax into an Alpha or Theta state (vs. normal or alert which is Beta)*

3. *Let your thoughts calm down until your ordinary mind starts racing; if blocked, try counting backward from 100 (José Silva)*

4. *If a thought is nagging at you, question if it's true (Byron Katie); watch your thoughts race by and know, "I am not them."*

5. *Start to visualize what you want to happen precisely as if you are experiencing or have already experienced it*

6. *Feel a deep sense of gratitude; even state out loud all the things you're grateful for, e.g., "I AM grateful for my health."*

7. *Use I AM statements, affirmations, and Ho'oponopono while listening to Solfeggio frequencies, Om chants, and visualizing to tune out the chatter of the thoughts swarming around your mind (grow still within)*

8. *Rinse and repeat until your desired picture imprints to the level that you can recall this later in your waking life at any moment (aka regroove your brain's neuroplasticity / teach your synapses to fire in a new array)*

Note: Do this upon waking or before bed. Avoid coffee or caffeinated tea that sets your mind into Beta mode, as you'll be too alert to achieve the altered states necessary to reprogram your subconscious mind most effectively.

Eventually, you'll reach a level where a negative thought or self-limiting belief enters your mind, and you just laugh at it, force shields up, and condition your mind to reject that negativity. "It's just a thought. It's not me. It's not true or real."

Now, you are empowered and maintaining a higher frequency vibration as a being around the clock, altering your chronic emotional tone and life state. Watch your feelings; they tell you your frequency. A lower emotional state causes your body's aura to emit lower-frequency energy waves, and the world reflects them back in infinite patterns of negative circumstances and coincidences. Bad luck!

You can be chaotically out of alignment or peacefully in tune and harmony. The choice is yours. Anger and fear jam the signal, creating distortions in the quantum field (your aura), blocking your higher self from synchronizing with the ONE mind that is ALL: infinite energy and infinite possibility. If bad things keep happening in your life, assess the frequency linked to that. What is the lesson, the gift, or the sign?

At any moment, you're a nanosecond away from taking the limitless pill. We are created with free will. And all we must do to change our lives is simply *decide* with intention. Why not make a new decision right now? I guess that's why they call the movement "New Thought."

Tone Zone:

432Hz is a frequency believed to be divine by many. According to Tesla, it is God's frequency and is said to resonate from within the Earth. Listening to this frequency allows you to connect with the universe and experience spiritual growth, emotional healing, love, and compassion.

432Hz can help you experience harmony, forgiveness, and deeper connection with others. It can also promote self-acceptance, healing of emotional wounds, and clearer thinking. This frequency induces a relaxed, calm, focused mindset, heightened creativity, inspiration, and reduced stress.

Listening to this frequency can help you align with the golden ratio (phi) and embrace fractal harmonic resonance. Unite your conscious understanding with subconscious intuition, fostering a deeper connection with inner wisdom and creative flow.

Research suggests that listening to 432Hz can promote physical healing by aligning with the body's inherent bioelectromagnetic field. This resonant harmony between the frequency and the body's energy systems can promote well-being. Improve your well-being, reduce stress, promote better sleep, reduce heart rate, and stimulate positive thinking.

The 528Hz Miracle Tone, known as the love frequency, is a powerful tool used in ancient religious chants and part of the original 6 Solfeggio frequencies. Opening the heart chakra profoundly impacts DNA, leading to healing and cellular repair within the body. 528Hz is linked to the sun's sound and has a mathematical connection to critical concepts such as Pi and Phi.

In addition to its healing properties, the 528Hz frequency can improve cognition, giving you clearer thinking and inner peace. It has emotional and spiritual benefits, promoting positive energy, love, and profound inner transformation. When used in meditation, it can foster self-empowerment and heightened spiritual connection, leading to personal growth and well-being.

Not only that, but the 528Hz frequency can also cleanse polluted environments and restore balance to the ecosystem, enhancing the vitality of flora and fauna. It is just one of the 9 Solfeggio frequencies, each with unique benefits. If you want to utilize them wisely, read up on their origins and implications.

What I love most about the 528Hz frequency is that it promotes self-love during meditation, reduces anxiety, and increases cell life. Could it even enhance longevity?

"I discovered Justin as my LinkedIn feed was full of glowing references from his clients. Justin is known as the master of Outbound Sales and building Pipeline with his modern human-and-technology-centric methods and he lived up to his reputation. Not only has Justin enabled me to secure meetings

with 18 prospects after only one month of coaching, but some of those prospects closed within days of launching my coaching business, and more will close in the future. But Justin is so much more than a Sales Coach; he's helped me believe in the value of my brand, and he helped me launch my business. Always available and responsive, he dives deep into complex challenges and teaches you how to create value at every opportunity and overcome the toughest obstacles. I'll be working with Justin again in the future, that is for sure. If you are a seller, a business leader, or founding a coaching/consultancy business - Justin's coaching is an investment you can't afford NOT to make." – Aaron Norris

CHAPTER 3

The myth of willpower

"Having a superpower has nothing to do with the ability to fly or jump, or superhuman strength. The truest super-powers are the ones we all possess: willpower, integrity, and most importantly, courage."

– Jason Reynolds

Quentin Tarantino writes scripts floating in his pool. Look into brain imaging studies by Dr. Nancy Andreasen, who describes these states as "free-floating periods of thought" essential to the creativity, innovation, and discoveries of Einstein, Edison, Mozart, and Da Vinci. Edison even fished without bait to free up his thoughts, which ensured no one bothered him.

The myth of willpower is a paradox. I always say, "If you have the will, I can teach you the skill." But that does not mean "muscling" or "straining" forward to achieve your goals. It truly means a desire aligned with your laser-focused, visualized goals and higher purpose. Seek to glorify God and serve others. When I finally lost the profit motive, I unleashed an incredible influx of abundance, sales, and clients because that altruism to serve radiated outwardly.

The mind, in its most relaxed state, effortlessly creates magic. From your inner stillness, dreams manifest; the formless gets thrown into form. That's where the power of Eckhart Tolle's work is so mighty: "the power of now." I love how Michael Neall interprets the Three Principles as "We are living in the feeling of our thinking." To become happy, we must first decide to be happy, and happiness finds us.

Henry David Thoreau wrote, "Happiness is like a butterfly, the more you chase it, the more it will elude you, but if you turn your attention to other things, it will come and sit softly on your shoulder."

Forcing your mind to stay positive is very hard, and you will become fatigued.

Wearing a mask of positivity will drain you. Maintaining special hours to do affirmations will sink you because the rest of your time, you are contradicting how you program your subconscious. Negativity rushes back in.

> *"Men of genius are sometimes producing most when they seem least to labor, for their minds are then occupied in the shaping of those conceptions to which they afterward give form." – Leonardo da Vinci*

You need to BE your true self 24/7. By returning to your inner being, inner knowing, and inner seeing, you will radiate outwardly from that knowingness, impacting your doing and thinking. That's the simplicity. I'm helping my coaching clients shift their inner being to the most confident version of themselves, that infinite multi-faceted capability forever realizing itself as you strive for goals in this lifetime.

The excuses and reasons fall away when you know that *you* are all you've got in this lifetime. You are worthy of wealth, promotion, unique genius, elevation, transcendence, and the achievement of any goal that you can believe. It goes back to Napoleon Hill, "What the mind can believe, you will receive."

I don't focus on self-discipline because this becomes a crutch. And I know there are a lot of "discipline = freedom" junkies that will fight me on this—more power to them. Jocko Willink's work is powerful. I'm not denying you must take action, but you can't whip your psyche into submission through abusiveness like a scene in *Drumline*.

Love yourself. Be love.

Love is an infinite force that requires no force at all. Sit back, relax, listen to music that aligns your chakras and DNA, and let your mind's eye harmonize with your truth. See it, and know it is for you. And fall headlong into pronoia: "The universe is plotting to do me good," you must think. Have you got chronic negative thoughts that minimize you? That's not the real you. It never could be.

Nikola Tesla knew:

> *"If you want to find the secrets of the universe, think in terms of energy, frequency, and vibration. The day science begins to study non-physical phenomena, it will make more progress in one decade than in all the previous centuries of its existence."*

By picturing yourself as a new identity repeatedly, you shift into it. Remember, 95% of your experience on this plane is subconscious. Your conscious awareness is just giving instructions to power the machine. You must always live in the feeling of the deeper identity you desire, grateful for that reality, even if it's not appearing in your present life as yet. You erase time if you can be thankful for things and know you ARE them before they arrive. You make a quantum leap.

"You become what you think about most of the time."
– Brian Tracy

Aristotle said, "We are what we repeatedly do. Excellence, then, is not an act but a habit." We are what we repeatedly think. *Creating* is a better term than acquiring customers. If we doubt our ability to attract a client or close a deal, we invariably will sow the seeds of doubt into the prospect's mind. That's suddenly a physical reality. Sales is the transference of belief; never doubt.

Read James Allen's masterpiece *As a Man Thinketh*, which hugely influenced Tony Robbins. The best way to reverse an unhealthy obsession is to out-create it and to turn all your inward energy and attention to something else: *service.*

Everyone in the sales training racket is rushing around with tactics, strategies, methods, and processes, trying to change the outer world to gain an external result. That's why most sales training fails! Everything you seek is an inside job. Shift your inner world, identity, and perception of your ability, and you will achieve a new paradigm.

Your comfort zone is strong. It holds you where you are today like quicksand. We can never get enough of what we don't want. (Dyer) All the gold is on the other side of fear. I'm pushing clients to seek what's uncomfortable and holding them accountable to get started doing it today. Break the chains off and get out of that rut. "But that sounds like willpower and strain, Justin?" It's a paradox.

Once you realign who you are with your true desires and eliminate internal value conflicts, you can harmonize with your true purpose, and this 'striving toward the goal' will build up the inertia you need to overcome any roadblocks your ego will throw in front of you.

Tony Robbins describes building self-esteem this way: "What makes you happy is the person you become in pursuit of those goals. We are made to either grow or die; there's no in-between. The *progress* is what makes you feel alive. Your brain starts to have inner pride, not fake ego pride. When you grow, you have something to give, and what makes people fulfilled is growing and giving, sharing it with somebody."

I used to *take* things from people. I was always taking, but then I realized the secret to life and happiness is *giving*. Talk about a polarity shift. It's harder to do than the simplicity of how it sounds.

> *"This is what I find most magnetic about successful givers: they get to the top without cutting others down, finding ways of expanding the pie that benefit themselves and the people around them. Whereas success is zero-sum in a group of takers, in groups of givers, it may be true that the whole is greater than the sum of the parts." – Adam Grant*

The opposite of happiness in French is boredom or ennui, not unhappiness. Napoleon Hill said, "Goals are dreams with a deadline," essential to our serenity.

EGO = Edge God Out (Dyer)

Per Emily Maroutian, "Ego is the process of disconnecting with the creative, true force of the universe. It is the process of making you separate from it, others, nature, and the universe."

Humility is power. Serving is power.

The more success you have, the more your ego will get out of the way. It blocks you repeatedly as you summit each peak, breakthrough after breakthrough. But one day, you can tame it. It starts with the decision to be aware of it. To see it for what it is. It's a lie, not you.

That's the paradox with very successful, egotistical people. Something broke down there. If you gain the world through arrogance, competition, or control, you've failed before you started. I love the concept in Wattles, "be creative, never competitive." Jeff Bezos said it best, "If we can keep our competitors focused on us while we stay focused on the customer, ultimately, we'll turn out all right."

Tony Robbins doesn't need clients; he charges one million per year for one-on-one coaching. It's pretty funny how humble David Beckham is in his Netflix documentary, and he's the GOAT. He doesn't need to remind you.

I've used these "attraction selling" processes to generate millions in income, attract multiple publishing deals, publish a #1 bestselling book series, and scale companies. Stadiums of sellers utilize the *JMM*™ to drive billions in pipeline on every continent. That line started as an affirmation and became true after freely distributing *the Codices* to Reddit.

"Imagination is more important than knowledge." Einstein believed this because what we see in our mind's eye just before sleeping, what we imprint into our deepest subconscious, becomes our reality. And from the universal oneness, we can tap into infinite imagination.

That's why Edison went fishing without bait, to be *still* and think deeply, tapping into a deeper creative force beyond himself and even time. He also took frequent naps and often sourced his most remarkable inventions and ideas in this relaxed state.

So listen to your body and take frequent naps. Go for long walks, toes in the dirt to feel the Earth's song or Schumann resonance. Yes, it even emits a healing frequency. Recharge your battery because there's magic in between waking and sleeping states. A restful brain fires at a far higher capacity.

When we grow before age 7, we develop many value conflicts based on how our teachers, grown-ups, and parents shape our experience and teach us to limit ourselves, trying to educate and groom us to be well-adjusted citizens. Clients are haunted by, "It's wrong for me to express myself because it's rude." "Money is the root of all evil." "Whenever I put myself out there, I'll be made fun of." "I will fail if I give this my all." "They're all going to laugh at me."

Our logical mind can see this is BS, but it still holds us back like the baby elephant on the post. It grows old and doesn't snap the line because it remembers it's tied. I loved this metaphor from Canfield, so I am bringing it up again to make a point as we seek to heal our inner child, causing distortions in our field.

How I interpret it is to understand that what we believe we can't do is probably a signpost to what we should do. I waited until I was 40 to write a book, but my 3rd-grade teacher, Mrs. Shupe, told me I was the most gifted writer she'd ever encountered in 30 years of teaching thousands of students.

When you genuinely hold the vision of something you desire and the wish fulfilled, you gain infinite energy toward the goal. It never feels like work. It flows like water; it gives you energy. You go into a flow state, and time flies. Soon, you see signs everywhere and synchronicities. Bizarre circumstances suddenly line up for you in no time. The natural order of paradise or God's timing ensues.

I'll breathe deep when I'm off the path or going negative. I'll look at one negative thought and dissect it. I'll understand it's not me. I may even smile slightly. I'll question it. Only then will I get back to the vision of the life I want to see in the now. You can't live in the past, you can't regret, you can't blame, you can't resent.

Let all that garbage go - decide to do it now.

Dwell on your past triumphs, not tragedies.

I couldn't meditate until I found cymatics, Solfeggio frequencies, and sonic waves that would naturally relax my brain into an Alpha and Theta state from the chronic caffeinated Beta place where I always developed business in beast mode.

These days, I feel more like a Shaolin monk. Rise and grind is now rise and relax the mind. Frank Zappa nailed Mindfulness: "A mind is like a parachute. It doesn't work if it is not open."

Relax! Sit and meditate to sacred music and think of every deal you closed, every promotion you got, everything in your career that went right. That will attract more of it energetically to you. Walk through the sequence of events in a sales cycle you want to see from the outcome achieved *backward*, reverse engineering all the steps you'll need to take along the way.

If you have a sales manager breathing down your neck, a conflict with a client or colleague, or somebody toxic in your space, I will surprise you with what I recommend. Bless them and run the Ho'oponopono process on them: "I'm sorry, I love you, please forgive me, thank you." We store up so much negative energy in these dramas that they are useless in the final analysis of life. Is it worth affecting your health and taking years off your life over something so minor and petty in retrospect?

The story goes that a billionaire was on his deathbed, and his mentee asked him, "Of all the things you worried about in this life, how many of them came true?" "Not even 1%," he replied."

Do you want to scale your business faster? Do the unscalable. Do you want to move faster in this life? Slow down. Power is still like a calm lake before you skip a stone and send ripples. Your mind is the lathe of God, the cosmic rudder commanding your inner faculties to produce any result you desire. The Emerald Tablet hid the secret, "As above, so below. As within so without."

People come to me wanting to make 7-figures, scale up to ten million dollars ARR, and shoot the lights out in one year. But all the outward success and rushing around they are seeking would be solved far more quickly, slowing way down.

> *"We overestimate what we can accomplish in one year but underestimate what we'll do in ten." – Marc Benioff*

I am focused on delivering exceptional value to *one* client at a time, giving meaningfully, and touching a life. Per Steve Chandler, "pluralism" is folly. When I get ahead of myself and start rushing around, I remember Steve's good little garden snail metaphor and slow down. Want a flood of customers? Focus on just ONE and give them your all. Transform their business. Their testimonials and referrals are a faster, more sustainable way to grow your own profitably.

Reminder: you're reading a book now from a record-breaking outbound sales hunter who was nicknamed "honey badger," "hummingbird," "Salesborg," and "the machine." Oh, how the mighty fall! But back then, I used to earn a lot less, work a lot more, and make far less impact. Riddle me that.

The "list is indeed the strategy," per Joey Gilkey. Storytime: I won't reveal who this rep is, but he's a friend and a champion – just look at that connect rate. He asked me, "What about avoiding burnout on the phones? I'm dialing 9-4 every day with no breaks. I'd be lying if I didn't say that grinding can be brutal sometimes. I only keep my head up by knowing it's a golden experience. Nine hundred dials last week at a 30% connect rate."

My answer: Flow state. Curiosity. Being fully present. The zen of "chop wood, carry water."

You need to pivot your cold call opening technique to "route ruin multiply" (RRM in Codex 7 & 13) instead of expected permission-based openers (PBOs) that lower status, such as, "Did I catch you at a bad time?" Hence, your tone remains calm-neutral; an air traffic controller with a Department of Motor Vehicles (DMV) matter-of-factness, asking open questions and learning about people, curiosity forward. Again, it's about making it an effortless conversation and conserving your vocal chords. That's how you can make large dialing days sustainable.

Also, remember the power of inertia. An object at rest stays at rest. An object in motion conversely stays in motion—Newton's 1st law.

Once you get started dialing, it snowballs downhill. That's why the heaviest weight you'll ever lift is the door to the gym. If you dread cold calling and procrastinate, traditional PBOs – permission-based openers – will be too much of a heavy lift. Traditionally, when you pitch up front, you get many hard rejections. In contrast, using Route-Ruin-Multiply (RRM), you trigger the Good Samaritan in the prospect, and they make many referrals immediately. Way less stressful! It's more like Aikido than "fast hands" Kung Fu. Read *Sales Superpowers: JMM 1.0* for more on effective cold-calling techniques.

"You can make more friends in two months by becoming interested in other people than you can in two years by trying to get other people interested in you." – Dale Carnegie

Your addictions rule you: a massive blind spot for most people. They believe they can't change. They've bought into "their story," their excuses, and the linear timeline of what happened to them. It's no secret: we all have trauma. Our past mistakes and circumstances outside our control haunt us all.

Step one: stop blaming yourself, forgive yourself. Trust that God put these circumstances into your life to make you wiser and teach you. If something truly awful happened to you, this process is way more complex, and you may be an innocent bystander. I'm not disputing that.

But the Canfield or Kight success formula remains the same: E+R = O - events + responses = outcome. We can't always control events; we can influence them by tapping into parallel universes in real time with the power of intention. However, many times, "letting go and letting God" and giving up trying to control and micromanage everyone in your path are the first stepping stones to freedom.

Chris Russell writes, "Nailed this, my friend. It's in the same vein as the Stoic mindset of only being able to control our response to events, not the events themselves.

We're hardwired to react in certain ways, and often, that's not something we can alter, but we can consciously choose how we respond after a reaction.

If we put ourselves in a scary situation, we are still going to feel 'oh sh$#' initially - our amygdala gets triggered. But we learn to counter it and respond how we want to, not how we automatically feel we should."

"It's your attitude, not your aptitude, that will determine your altitude," per Zig Ziglar. We can only control how we respond. The R Factor dictates new outcomes or how we respond to events we can't control in that equation.

Your brain has neuroplasticity; it's clay. Maxwell Maltz said it takes 21 days to break a habit. James Clear challenges that notion, "The honest answer is: forever. Because once you stop doing it, it is no longer a habit. A habit is a lifestyle to be lived, not a finish line to be crossed. Make small, sustainable changes you can stick with."

People who have smoked their entire life can suddenly rewire their brains, and they do it by coming to a new understanding. But why have a scare with emphysema or lung cancer before making the change? My mentor had a widowmaker block, a 98% clogged artery, and nearly died. He resumed living from an enlightened place and is wiser now, but he told me, "I should have lived as I do now before the block." Hindsight is 20/20.

"When we take things for granted, they get taken from us." – Rhonda Byrne

We all take our lives for granted in some way, big or small. We are diminishing our power to change by believing we are stuck. If someone held your head underwater, how violently would you throw them off you to breathe? Picture a woman lifting a car off her baby. We hear these stories of sheer mental intensity in a crisis producing physical strength. David Goggins teaches us that we use minimal physical and mental capacity.

I worked with a powerlifting coach. First, he taught me not to fear 300 pounds. Secondly, he taught me techniques to get all the muscle groups under the weight. Thirdly, I had a weight belt and did a lot of stretching. We worked up to one rep very slowly, but once I got there, I was fearless. I was confident I could do it because he could do 500 pounds or something insane. So, my mindset allowed me to handle that once daunting weight in a very short period.

Apply this metaphor to anything. My desire to get strong, to learn to master that fear, to change my physical reality, and to understand the impact on my mentality got me out of my comfort zone. I leaped!

Sellers I coach boil over with logical excuses. They didn't have enough money, didn't get the training, grew up poor; and their father said, "If you get successful, your marriage will fall apart." Many were bullied, picked on, and have crushing student debt. Over time, their invisible income ceiling silently forms and appears solid to them. But you can shatter it.

You can change your habits by rewiring your brain and subconscious mind, creating new neural pathways. You can start to see the 70,000 thoughts you have daily as something separate from you. Usually, when you abuse your body or mind, there's a recurring thought sitting there. If you see it, question why it's true á la Byron Katie, and let it go, a miracle occurs. There's finally free attention in your head to think the thoughts you want. You become someone who is BEING cigarette-free, healthy, a fanatical prospector, and loving and curious toward people again. New thoughts are not enough to change habits. Desire is not enough.

If you change who you are to pure compassion and someone treats you horribly on a cold call, instead of thinking, "What an awful person," you meet them with forgiveness, compassion, and empathy. "Wow, I bet they're having a brutal day." Who knows what kind of drama is going on in their life? Everyone is suffering. Everyone is fighting a unique battle you can't see.

The enlightened rep lets this go, forgives, or, as Jesus walked, never even condemns them in the first place. It's just the nature of this pale blue-collar job: you're soliciting. They kicked the cat. You're the messenger they shot today. And on you go to the next call, the following outreach, with a pure heart, zen attitude, and open mind to serve.

I finally conquered my procrastination to prospect with an elementary understanding. What have I done every last day of my life since I was young: sick, healthy, rich, poor, stressed, calm, traveling? Brush my teeth, shower, sleep, eat, etc. If the most fundamental habit in being successful in sales is prospecting, what if I did this every day, seven days per week?

What if I could learn to love, be obsessed, and addict myself to it? What if it came to me as natural as breathing, and I enjoyed it as much as sipping chamomile tea? I've rewired my psyche to do this fanatically. Now, I associate prospecting with service, talking to amazing people I can help, radiating love, and changing lives, hearts, and minds. I love to do it, frankly. I could do it all day; it feels like breathing to me.

My fallback mode is not Netflix. It's 4th frame conversation on LinkedIn.

Sales is a big drinking fest of happy hours, afterparties, Vegas, and events galore. Even in the digital sphere, it's all about mass networking via webinars and dark social Slack groups, drinking from the tap of amateurs masquerading as gurus.

I'm not judging the drinkers out there. I just can't think of lucrative business deals that go down after four stiff drinks.

Nothing good happens after midnight or in the middle of a one-sided webinar on LinkedIn with the same 50 participants mingling in the comments.

You need to decide on a healthy lifestyle most conducive to giving you the stamina and mental fortitude required to achieve your goals. Alcohol interferes with the brain's communication pathways, throwing it out of balance. Alcohol can impact your natural dopamine production as all drugs do, giving you temporary hits or feelings of relaxation or relief. If you drink enough, you just go into the deep subconscious mode, not the healing kind in this book, and pass out animalistically.

440Hz tuned music has only been the standard since 1939, so the radio and Spotify put you into focus modes of dissonance while coffee over-focuses you, causing Beta brainwaves. Drugs spike your dopamine and serotonin, and then your neurotransmitters that naturally create the feel-good chemicals don't fire the way you used to. The lows are even lower. Trying to work after two glasses of wine is possible, but you're unlikely to think clearly. Where am I going with this?

1. Drink more water and tea, watch the caffeine, and make it herbal even if green tea has anti-oxidants because this book is about achieving the Alpha and Theta states. Progression: Gamma > Beta > Alpha > Theta > Delta (sleep) - all the work we're doing is in the middle band.

2. Rise with the sun and walk out on a beach or trail with your feet in the dirt soil or grass. Ground yourself.

3. Make sure you limit caffeine, drugs, and alcohol when you do the process of *Musifestation* so it can work faster for you. Eat healthier like your "vegetarian grandmother" from farm to table.

4. Breathe: I can't tell you how many people, even on a phone call, breathe jaggedly, sucking for air. Work on regulating your breathing so you breathe fully. Try Kundalini fire breathing (hat tip Dhiren Desa), Wim Hof ice bathing, or Zen meditation: anything that can give you more control over your breath.

5. Do this for 100 days, and you'll feel so good your neurophysiology will change (body, brain, and mind). You'll see massive increases in focus and the ability to create fast manifestation.

Generally, when humans are stressed, they take pills. They drink. They smoke. They complain and gossip, and they tap into the negative thought stream.

Try this. Next time you feel stressed, meditate on sacred music. Have some herbal tea and sip it. Count backward in your mind from 100. (Silva method)

What I do when I'm feeling depressed, down, or negative – which is rare these days – is I simply center my mind by thinking of a happy thought, something from the past, a cute animal, a sunset, or a person I love.

Then I repeat mantras in my mind, affirmations we've discussed here. I may carve out 5-10 minutes to reset to all 9 Solfeggio frequencies cycling through and focus on breathing. Try this: say, "I am love." Do some H'oponopono. "I love you, thank you, I'm sorry, please forgive me." In any order, think of what you want and say it. Joe Vitale called this "cleaning." To clear the body, clear the mind.

Go back to the last big win you had and rerun it. *The Power of Habit* by Charles Duhigg is a phenomenal book, and my takeaway is to set up a system of new rewards for your triggers rather than eating or drinking to feel relaxed. If you feel triggered by stress, jump on a Peloton or meditate.

Living in a building with a gym helps; putting a Peloton or yoga mat next to your bed helps. Feeling an addictive impulse and replacing it with a natural way to increase dopamine and serotonin is an excellent solution. Pain also releases dopamine, so that's where the runner's high or mental clarity from a heavy lift stems from.

After 10,000 steps or a light jog, my reward is a hot shower or a cold-pressed green juice. But then I get new cravings when I do this for a while because I'm reprogramming myself and the reward system. Negative associations are strong: frustration = overeat, pain = smoke, stress = drugs, anxiety = workaholic.

You'd get ahead if you tied these base impulses to movement. But to me, relaxing my mind and going into the alpha/theta state is an immediate stress reliever. I often work with sacred music because it slows me down, allowing me to focus and move one task at a time. Haste makes waste.

Remember, slowing down speeds you up, and doing what's unscalable scales up your business.

Instead of needing "clients," shed the plurality á la Steve Chandler. Slow down and serve one client the most powerfully ever. Do research on just one C-Level executive and write a handwritten note. Slow down and execute some Dale Dupree meets Stu Heinecke rebel contact marketing tactics like sending crumpled letters, cartoons starring your prospect, or cutting boards with a note that reads, "Can we carve out some time?"

Send a drone *without* the remote control (to receive only if they take a meeting) and drop off fresh-baked cookies that are still warm. I once heard a story of a rep who waited in a CEO's parking space with cupcakes. Make a donation to their favorite local charity on their behalf. Not everyone wants "stuff!"

If you slow down and think about what this person would *really* love and what would *actually* get their attention, you'll get farther at prospecting than blasting a thousand emails a day.

Changing Habits Exercise:

1. *Take anything you do that is self-destructive, and find the thought you had just before it.*

2. *Be witness to what triggers you and the reward. For example, the voice in your head could sound like: "I feel stressed, so I eat ice cream. I'm intimidated by prospective CEOs, so I just sit on social media in the feed instead of prospecting, putting it off for later."*

3. *Tie a new reward to the trigger by changing the channel: "I feel stressed; I'll pour some herbal tea and put on my favorite Toto song. I'm intimidated by prospects, so I'll pick up the phone **now** instead and use a ROUTE opener. I'll send an InMail to warm up this contact."*

4. *Habit stacking is an incredible hack. Listen to uplifting audiobooks while you work out. Are you stuck in an airport and can't prospect? Don't worry, be crappy. (Guy Kawasaki) Send invites on LinkedIn. Send humorous one-liners and GIFs to prospects first degree. Are you feeling burned out? Walk uphill on a treadmill instead of having another coffee and try to send personalized 1st-degree messages to the first ten prospects you see on LinkedIn.*

Your triggers may not change, but E + R = O is correct. Events + Responses = Outcomes (Canfield/Kight). Respond to the same trigger with a good habit and a new reward. You could eat a healthy salad instead of choosing your candy sugar rush to spike your energy temporarily before you crash. Instead of being frustrated and avoiding prospecting, find a fun, engaging way to simply "have conversations," seeing LinkedIn as the ultimate "24/7, always-on networking event."

"Every sale happens within a conversation." – Litvin / Chandler

Reframe the positive thing you don't want to do. I used to get up at 5 am and go for a run, and by not sleeping in, everything went better in my day. I rewarded myself with a hot bath and a protein shake and trained my brain to like that as much as waffles with maple syrup.

I used to get stuck in Atlanta airport during lightning storms with canceled flights. I trained my brain to enjoy noodling on the LinkedIn mobile app and having deep intellectual conversations with prospects that turned into Zoom calls in the DMs. "But how do you get them to talk to you, JM?" Curiosity and open questions. The more you invest in building the relationship upfront, the bigger the deal. (hat tip Alan Weiss)

CHAPTER 4

Hold your vision 24/7 for manifestation

"As you think, you travel, and as you love, you attract."

– Zen Proverb

I always struggled with meditation because I couldn't turn my brain off. I found much of the law of attraction very "kumbaya." Let's get out the acoustic guitars and gather around the bonfire. It wasn't hard-hitting enough for me. I was grossly mistaken.

I would look at other thought leaders, celebrities, millionaires, and billionaires and elevate them mentally on a pedestal as if they were somewhere out there, beyond me in another galaxy, not close by, not something in me that I could recognize and manifest.

When I had no choice but to hustle so hard and get myself out of debt, I did. When my back was against the wall, I always dug my way out rapidly. I found a compelling YouTube video entitled "How bad do you want it?" with 49 million views featuring Giavanni Ruffin from the Seattle Seahawks practicing. Listen to motivational speaker Eric Thomas sermonize over Giavanni's insane training regimen for pro football about holding your head underwater and how hard and violently you'd push to survive. He clarifies, "When you want success as bad as breathing, you will be successful." If this video doesn't motivate you, nothing will.

What's crazy about success is we all go 10X massive action in some areas. For many people, that's eating, drinking, watching Netflix, complaining, gossiping, doomscrolling, and all manner of vices. Let me be clear on this revelation: self-abuse, victimization, and chronic negative thoughts are vices. But logically, ask yourself, how does that serve you? Do you want a life of sympathy or success? Do you want to create abundance for your family and serve your community, charity, and church? Or struggle forever in sales.

The choice is yours today.

So, how do you shift that? Simple process. First, let your mind race in, and then start letting go of the negative thoughts and question them. See that they aren't you. You can listen to the angel on one shoulder or the devil on the other. You have free will.

> *"What you focus on grows, what you think about expands, and what you dwell upon determines your destiny." – Robin Sharma*

Secondly, flip every negative thought into a positive affirmation. Watch this, "I could never do that." "I can *build* that company." "I'm not good enough." "I am great." "I'll never get rich." "I am infinitely able to create abundance." "I'll never hit quota." "It's easy for me to hit quota here, and I'm grateful for the privilege."

You'll start just to see these negative thoughts come in and be able to clear them out by stating their inverse. Let the negativity be your fuel, turning it into gold: self-love and self-worth. Byron Katie and Curtis "50 Cent" Jackson inspired my thinking here.

Your affirmations will become mantras from the space this creates in your psyche. You'll be able to become a champion and lift rocks with the power of your mind, literally. Some say monks can really do this and even levitate. They can drastically change their body temperatures, channeling heat deep in meditation.

You may not be able to bend spoons or read minds, but the superpower you develop will be an unshakeable belief in yourself as you cultivate a healthy self-love. Your life will change if you repeatedly practice these techniques, from *acorns to oaks,* for 20-30 days. You'll start to see your sales performance, happiness, and even health turn around.

Weed the garden of your mind. Only the grateful mind attracts.

You are a magnet that attracts like things. Except the things you attract are based on your subconscious, deep-seated beliefs, not when awake. If you feel extroverted and happy, but the same problems keep showing up, there's gotta be something deep down that's out of alignment.

Sleep is so powerful because you can awaken the dreamer within. Neville Goddard had a process called the "pruning sheers of revision," where you relive the day as you would have ideally wanted it to go before you sleep. And that could be any reality you'd like. If you do that every day as you fall asleep, you will start to see astounding things happen in the ensuing days.

I keep sharing the Salvador Dali story of the metal plate he napped on while holding the key to clang on the metal as he moved between Beta, Alpha, and Theta states. He knew something about sleep and creativity! It's the same reason why hypnotism does work. Prince credits his prolific work ethic with respect for sleep, even installing a purple canopy bed in his recording studio. He recorded thousands of finished songs in his vault that are his legacy. [RIP]

The real law of attraction means wanting what you desire most for others. That's why prayer is so powerful, especially for other people. That's why *The Go-Giver* by Bob Burg and Zig Ziglar's philosophy of driving value for others is so key. Karma is real; paying it forward is real. When Rhonda emptied the ATM and gave from the bottom of her soul with tears in her eyes, it shifted the polarity of what she was pushing away and magnetized that exact thing toward her: riches and abundance.

If you want a business deal to go a certain way, tell yourself the story of the signed contract from the viewpoint that it has already happened. As Michael Beckwith said poetically, "The universe will correspond to the nature of your song."

When you are perplexed at the 11th hour because a prospect has ghosted you, the solution is not to start frantically calling them and acting desperate. Get very still, get into the visualization flow, and be in that relaxed state of effortless magic. Bless that person and pray for them. Feel the feelings of having sorted that out. You will get a random phone call, or some mysterious positive chain of events will happen.

Salespeople are driven by fear. They are often deadened inside to the point of apathy by constant rejection. Pessimistic and battle-hardened, we proudly develop a thick skin or mental callus to help us survive the next onslaught. But becoming jaded and cynical is not a badge of honor. Thinking like this will block you.

Respect your potential customers, even the nightmare ones. You need to cultivate a healthy love for yourself and compassion for other people. This will give you the empathy, emotional intelligence (EQ), and curiosity you need to crack the code of creating pipeline and income. The more interested in them you are, the more attractive you become.

Magnetics and polarity dictate all human systems and endeavors. When you want something badly, you are often pushing it away. BE it, don't want it. Let the desire become an inner knowing it is already yours.

When bad things happen in life, see it as a sign that you are still on the path. Trust in God that you are constantly being put in the exact position you need to be. Look for the lesson. Maybe you weren't meant to fly on a plane that day. Perhaps the detour you took is for some domino effect set of reasons you won't be able to see for months or even years.

That's why I always say, "See all things and situations from the viewpoint of advantage." That's the silver lining playbook. Returning to ancient zen, a pine tree snaps in a hurricane while a palm tree is flexible, bends, and lives - never uprooted in many storms.

You are unstoppable in your psychic energy when you become like water carving rock, persistent, chameleon, ever flowing and changing form. Bruce Lee, the greatest martial artist of all time, stated, "Be like water."

Mantra translates from Sanskrit as "a thought behind speech or action." It's something you repeat, chant, and engrain that merges with your identity. If you chanted "I'm unstoppable" all day, every day, in time, it would erode that brutal inner voice trying to convince you you're not good enough. Tony Robbins did.

One client asked me, "But isn't me being hard on myself what makes me so savage?" It's the opposite. There are only two forces in this world: fear and love. Fear is the mind-killer (I love *Dune* by Frank Herbert), causing negative experiences to cling to your low-frequency position.

Choose love. The more you love and *believe* in yourself 24/7, the more it will become your reality of life experience. Rhonda floored me with this hot take: "A notch above believing is *knowing,* and knowing is beyond the mind." From belief, love will manifest all around you. Goodness, good fortune, and God's grace. It's that simple. What are you thinking right now? How are you feeling? That's what's going to show up for you. Spend all day obsessing on deals you've already closed *in your mind*, not doubting whether they will.

If you're stuck and can't get out of your head, here's a straightforward thought process to dig out.

1. How am I feeling?

2. Wait, if I'm feeling bad, it must be what I'm thinking.

3. Is what I'm thinking true? "I can't do this." "I'm awful." "I always screw things up." (Byron Katie, *The Work),* or if you look at Syd Banks and *3 Principles* to see the "misunderstanding" occurring and realize it's just that.

4. Now, the more you look at thoughts and see that it's just erroneous thinking, the more you pull away into: "Wait, if I'm not my thoughts, my mind or body, what am I?"

5. You are a connection point to the universal mind, God, infinite energy, and creation. Beating yourself up all day verbally doesn't serve you - you must become only love.

6. Now, from this place of stillness that emerges when you see all the negative thoughts separate from yourself, start

to state what you are: "I am love." "I am wealth, health, abundance, and joy." "I am peace." "I am helping and serving others." "I am capable of anything I put my mind to." "I love myself and celebrate myself." "I am worthy of love." That's a big one.

My biggest block in 40 years and the essence of your biggest breakthrough in this book, in case you haven't had the light bulb go off yet?

"I am not my thoughts."

I'll challenge Goggins. Stay hard? The hardest humans who made the most positive change on this planet are also soft inside, like Gandhi, Mandela, MLK Jr., and the Dalai Lama, with a message of peace, unity, and love.

> *"My religion is very simple. My religion is kindness." -*
> *His Holiness the 14th Dalai Lama*

I realized that the self-limiting negative self-talk is just my subconscious lashing out. It's some trauma before I was 7. Psychotherapy helps us ease the sting of our past. But the present is a decision. Just knowing for certain that nothing bad you think about yourself can possibly be true will break the chains off your life.

The greatest warrior need not even go into battle as they've conquered their mind. Lao Tzu said, "Mastering others is strength. Mastering yourself is true power." Sun Tzu put it, "If you know the enemy and know yourself, you need not fear the result of a hundred battles."

My clients tell me, "I can't charge high fees." "I can't earn $300K, $500K, or a million dollars. I never will. I'm not you."

"I've tried everything, and I always fail because...." Excuses, excuses, excuses. They believe in their past. They believe in their victim story.

The greatest gift is that the present *is* the future. You can create a new future reality anytime by deciding in the present, grounding yourself, and filling your heart and mind with LOVE. That's the power of putting down your cross to bear and taking the monkey off your back.

I'd never seen this quote until recently. Werner Erhard states, "Create your future from your future." And I saw this in the work of Dan Sullivan and Dr. Benjamin Hardy. The hiring managers in tech companies always say, "Past performance determines the future," and 90% of companies hire based on this bias. And that's usually true because of an employee's comfort zone, habituation, and cyclical mindset. But you can create a new habit in 21 days. You can choose an infinite number of new futures by changing your beliefs.

Who are you being? What do you believe about yourself that is untrue and holds you back? NOTHING you think about yourself that is negative can be true. Sure, you could be behaving temporarily out of alignment with the truth, but chronically, all human beings, deep down, have the capacity for good and serving others.

This chapter is all about holding your vision 24/7. If you do the *Musifestation* process, you can anchor on that joyous feeling of your "wishes fulfilled" (Dyer/Neville). You can call forth a more robust internal frame when dealing with others. You'll develop unshakeable belief and confidence in yourself, making you fearless, bold, and dauntless - indefatigable.

Unshakeable belief gives you massive power.

When bad thoughts about yourself come in, disagree. Shoot them down. They will become trivial, popping like soap bubbles, and you'll laugh at them as pieces of your subconscious to discard, not even inner demons or mental flaws. They're not necessary anymore. Realize it's just your survival mechanism (ego) trying to protect itself from a saber tooth tiger. The ancient part of your brain reacts out of instinct and is useless to modern-day life.

Sometimes, you'll get a terrible rejection on the phone, in a job interview, or a deal you depended on will slip or stall. Your boss, colleague, or direct report will say something that upsets you. That's when you need to become grounded again. Nothing can hurt you that you don't let hurt you.

"We teach people how to treat us." – Dr. Phil

Everything appearing in your life is 100% manifesting from what's happening internally. I always caveat this because evil exists in the world, and some people are victims. However, most of what's happening to my clients in the working world and personal relationships is by their design, stemming from chronically misaligned thinking over many years.

Keep a journal and a dream board, and write goals and affirmations in the affirmative: I AM present tense or from the viewpoint of it already having happened. Be grateful as if the miracles you seek have already occurred. Know that you are worthy of anything you can see in this world. If someone else can do it, you can do it. I'm among the least qualified people in the world to earn seven figures. I went from the gutter to the stars, mainly wasting my God-given aptitudes in writing, communication, and selling. I could immediately hear a cacophony of positive voices when I realized I was blocking my gifts.

Epiphany: If I'm a genius in communication, what does that translate to? Well, maybe instead of following the David Sandlers of the world, I'll become one. I've always been savage at cracking "top of the funnel." What if I specialized in TOFU and built the most powerful communication system ever for effective client acquisition?

And that's the whole genesis of this series. But you could do that? What's your forte, your knack, your gift? Not just a talent that you are conquering with hard work. I truly believe everyone has a unique genius that they can tap into. I realize this challenges Carol Dweck, although a growth mindset is still helpful.

> *"Everybody is a genius. But if you judge a fish by its ability to climb a tree, it will live its whole life believing that it is stupid." – Einstein*

When I coach people, I see the gold in them; often, they cannot see. We find a way to help them monetize what they're best at and love the most. Most people overlook the inherent gifts they came into this world with, which I believe is the meaning of *The Alchemist* by Paulo Coelho. The treasure you seek is typically at your feet as you search the world. Only you can uncover the secrets of your own heart. So get quiet now and begin to listen.

> *"Ask what makes you come alive and go do it. Because what the world needs is people who have come alive." – Howard Thurman*

CHAPTER 5

The Power of Intention vs. Positive Thinking

"By banishing doubt and trusting your intuitive feelings, you clear a space for the power of intention to flow through."

— *Wayne Dyer*

People sense when you're inauthentic in selling, coaching, and consulting. When you're out for yourself, any mask you wear will eventually bite you. The methods in popular red sales books focus on getting you to memorize scripts, templates, and clever manipulations. But you're not an actor, and life is not a dress rehearsal.

What if you shift who you are *being* and your intention toward the other person? I'll never forget a rep who tried everything to land meetings, and nothing worked.

Contrary to the misinterpreted *Challenger Sale* mentality of playing "hard to get," his manager simply told him, "Why don't you show them you care." And voilà, deals started to open and close for him. First, align your true intention for serving your clients powerfully. Assess your inner knowing that you have intrinsic value just showing up in someone's life. Then, get present with your belief in your solution, technology, chosen company, the people you represent, and the caliber of quality delivery. It develops unstoppable courage within you.

I interrupt strangers intending to "transform their business." I'll never forget that Tom Radlism. When they object or reject, I meet that with understanding and love and press a bit firmer, breaking through their resistance and often multiple "Nos." I express how others I've helped rejected me initially and commiserate with their skepticism.

I feel morally and ethically righteous to sell to people or enroll people. Why? My techniques will help them earn hundreds of thousands, even millions, over their lifetime. So I press on where others fold. And this "intention" signals leadership. It's not pushy; it's in their interest.

Sales is the "transference of belief." I love the old proverb: The IASM in ENTHUSIASM is "I am sold myself." It's another classic Zig Ziglar. I think I heard it somewhere from Cardone.

Expectation is the most potent part of the secret. When you expect positive things to happen, you are spurred into massive action and act accordingly. When I wanted to release a metaphysical sales book, I went to many publishers and got rejected. I held the vision of exactly how I wanted to do it until I met Jeremy Jones, who shared my sense of urgency around releasing the "ChatGPT whispering" insights that have been the hallmark of my work today at the forefront of the AI selling revolution.

"Where focus goes, energy flows. And where energy flows, whatever you're focusing on grows. In other

words, your life is controlled by what you focus on. That's why you need to focus on where you want to go, not on what you fear." – Tony Robbins

I wanted to do a book series that would resonate and sell at the Challenger, SPIN, and GAP levels. It was high time to codify my outbound methods into an operating system that would help millions of sellers and leave a legacy for many generations to come.

I expected I'd secure this book deal and put it out immediately. I expected it would debut at the top on Amazon. I expected it would be life-changing for people to read it. And that's what happened to the tee. In my mind's eye, I never saw anything else but all my books as #1. I've since received over 500 5-star reviews. Both new books held the top spots in the world for months.

When I initially sat in Silicon Valley with $2K to my name, visualizing $100K, I imprinted a new reality so heavily on my subconscious mind with *Musifestation* that I didn't even realize I'd shifted into a new universe.

Expecting a 10X outcome isn't conceited. It isn't narcissism. It's a healthy self-love. That's why I always ask clients about the goal behind their goals. (Chandler) That's your *why* and what's driving you. Taking massive action creates self-esteem because it merges with your reward expectation.

"Never allow thoughts of doubt to enter your mind. Be aware when negative thoughts come and stop them in their tracks." – Rhonda Byrne

Cast down all doubt in yourself. All doubt is a lie. The setbacks you experience are there to teach you lessons. That's why the Khalil Gibran quote is a big reveal. "Out of suffering have emerged the strongest souls; the most massive characters are seared with scars."

Expect a check or promotion, live in the bigger house, drive a better car, and receive the commission check before closing the sale. Expectation equals: God is good, and I believe I am worthy. For many of you reading this, it's too far of a leap. You must remember I barely eked by check to check for most of my twenties. I needed a degree, experience, connections, or prospects.

How did I get started? I found a tech incubator and worked for a couple of companies doing marketing and sales on pure commission. I also got to know the VCs in my town by helping them fundraise for their charity events. Then, I launched my own masquerade ball series. By putting myself in the orbit of high-powered people, I gained new pathways to prosperity via networked intelligence.

One of the best ways to improve your future is to raise your standards. Don't settle for mediocre. Don't settle to be surrounded by energy vampires. Raise your standards. Demand a better life for yourself. Even if it's impossible now, putting that pressure on your self-image, self-esteem, and identity creates leverage. Now you've decided to make a change. Now, you can think of new thoughts leading to a new life.

If you are unhappy or depressed, if you hate your job. Learn to serve.

"If you want to feel connected to your own purpose, know this for certain: Your purpose will only be found in service to others, and in being connected to the something far greater than your mind/body/ ego." – Wayne Dyer

Genuinely selling from the heart and soul expresses giving, and your outer identity sheds like a snake's skin. You disappear into a light beam of curiosity pointed at the prospect. True orientation toward others dissolves negative self-talk, insecurity, fear, and worry like springtime sun on a snowmelt.

People ask me how to run a discovery or closing call or what to say at the beginning of almost any sales situation. The secret is I just place all my attention on the other person, and the rest takes care of itself. I knew what to say flawlessly from that operating system when I became genuine, compassionate, and curious. It's not about the scripts, frameworks, templates, or heuristics (mental shortcuts) at this selling level. You are two humans: *being*. You see them for who they truly are. You dig to the root, you help - you serve.

We experience many negative thought forms in sales. The antidote to apathy, depression, and losing motivation is to attach yourself to a mission greater than yourself. (Of course, I respect if it's clinical, so get professional help.)

The profit motive is a mind-killer.

When the customer senses commission breath, you are dead in the water. So simply shifting your intention to altruism already sends another subconscious signal as you show up differently. "Most experts agree that 70 to 93% of communication is nonverbal." (Pauline Ashenden) If 95% of your subconscious influences your actions, then surface changes of templates, scripts, and pitching tonality do very little. Perhaps this sentence is the most crucial in the book.

Physical signals also shift by shifting our identity. Being and consciousness influence our behaviors, mannerisms, and outer tonality. And that's why a solid understanding of frames is so vital.

Frames are talked about at great length by my friend Oren Klaff. Whoever has the more powerful frame when they collide in interpersonal relationships, dating, and meetings will always win.

What you believe and chronically say about yourself becomes your story. Your negativity becomes your self-fulfilling prophecy. What prophecy will you write for your life?

Sublimation: this means taking one impulse and turning it into another. You are not a beast.

> *"You are an infinite spiritual being having a temporary human experience." – Wayne Dyer*

Take your aggression, negative impulses, survival mechanisms, frustrations, and sexual energy and sublimate them. Modify any base impulses into building momentum in the creative process. Put all your pent-up intensity into your work and mission of service. Transmute the chaos of being human into the gold of building, creating, striving, and succeeding, climbing one mountain after another.

Kevin Costner got it right: "Nothing's free in *Waterworld*." Such is the human experience. There's no such thing as a free lunch. Everyone is acting in their own interest. When you realize that, understanding sales and human nature becomes pretty simple. But can *you* give without a hook on the other end? Be the exception to that rule. Pay it forward without expecting anything in return. Count your blessings and take nothing for granted. That's the doorway to miracles.

Life is about the journey, not the destination, so Carpe Diem: seize the day. Or, as I like to say, Carpe Noctem: seize the night.

What won't work:

- "Talking the talk" about things you'll do and dreams you'll achieve without "walking the walk."
- Creating vision boards and affirmations can be helpful, but it won't be enough if you don't take persistent action.
- Viewing your goals as something you'll achieve someday is a limiting mindset that will only hold you back. As Yoda once said, "Try not, do."
- It's equally flawed to be vague about what you want; it will limit or confuse the universe, ending in only partial manifestation. Specificity is your roadmap to abundance.
- Change is impossible if you're negative most of the time but only sporadically think and do what's right. Live your life as if your words and thoughts are being streamed onto the big monitor in Times Square 24/7.
- Holding onto hate, fear, anger, or resentment is futile. Abusing yourself or others is a sin, even thinking about it. The dark side (devil) will tempt you and trick you. Stay in the light. I am the light bringer in a world of dark gurus.
- Refusing to love yourself blocks growth. LOVE is where all your power comes from.

What will work:

- Make a detailed list of all your goals and create a file (doc, slide, Canva) with a vivid picture of you achieving them.
- Believe (think, speak, and act) as if you have already achieved your goals and get the "abundance feeling."
- Spend 30 minutes daily journaling, visualizing, and expressing gratitude for the goal you have achieved.

- Wish the same for others.

- Trust your gut; it'll point you to the exact tactics and strategies necessary to hit your goal. (Luckily, I wrote *JMM 1.0* and *2.0* loaded with methods for full-cycle selling that will carry you rapidly to explosive pipeline and revenue.)

- Channel aggression, frustration, and any negative feelings into positive activities: prospecting, meridian tapping, cycling, Reiki energy work, hiking, journaling, working out, kickboxing, meditation, cooking, deep breathing, going for long, brisk walks on the beach (feet in the sand - study "grounding" or "earthing"), playing or listening to music, etc.

- Change your geography and surround yourself with positive people; block/remove toxic people from your life. (The wealthier you get, the more extensive your block list; just ask Marc Andreessen.)

- Cultivate the feeling of deep and constant gratitude, and give thanks through prayer. If you wish to be forgiven, *forgive*. If you wish to be loved, *love*. The world is a mirror reflecting back at you what you are putting out into it.

- Say "No" more frequently and guard your time. Stop letting people use you.

Thank you, Aaron Norris, for your insights into the above. He's a talented coach specializing in bringing work-life balance to sellers' lives as he rose up the ranks quickly inside Amazon AWS.

Troubleshooting:

What won't work for people is keeping the same burnt-out friends who hold them down, maintaining an unhealthy lifestyle, and drinking nightly. Generally, drugs, food, and alcohol are all escapist. Violent TV - do you notice "Netflix and Chill" has become endless formulaic action movies NSFW?

We are what we repeatedly ingest. Fill your mind with constructive content. Salespeople spend way too much time reading sales books! Go out and experience life, and you'll gain *true grit.* (hat tip, Scott Leese) Learn from the greats who lived before you. There are a million biographical audiobooks (I highly recommend Walter Isaacson's), documentaries from Ken Burns, movies like *The Pursuit of Happyness,* and classics like *Rocky* or *Chariots of Fire.* I'm digging the docuseries on Sly and Arnold. Brené Brown's TED Talk on vulnerability as courage is epic. Catch *Stutz* by Jonah Hill and Tony Robbins's *I'm Not Your Guru.*

Watch content that inspires and uplifts you, like live talks by Michael Neill, Eckhart Tolle, and Byron Katie. Read biographies of people who made it against all odds or struggled far greater than you'll ever know. It will give you a new perspective. (E.g., *Man's Search for Meaning* by Viktor Frankl, who survived the concentration camps by mastering his mind.) In the introduction, I've mentioned a slew of resources that influenced this book.

Seek out and spend time with mentors in the real world. Emulate what they do. Sales is a trade skill and apprenticeship. If you want to upskill with live role plays and drills, go to HardSkill. Exchange and sign up for some coaching.

One last tip from Alex Hormozi that I agree with is scanning many books or reading just the first 30 pages. When something truly resonates, get the book on Audible and in print formats, reading it 5X until it sinks in. The litmus test for theoretical knowledge retention is that you can thoroughly apply it in your field. It's an honor that people approach my work in this way. It's a best practice I model with my favorite authors.

What are the top 10 biggest reasons people don't attract what they truly want in their lives?

1. They sporadically envision a new reality vs. constantly. You won't BECOME your dream if you never shift your 95% subconscious identity. Deep down, there is creeping doubt somewhere in your heart of hearts.

2. They envision themselves getting there *someday*.

3. They don't cultivate gratitude and act *as if* they've already received their desires.

4. They don't believe in themselves (hidden imposter syndrome) and have low self-esteem – a good coach can help you with that, as will many exercises in this book.

5. Doing one thing and thinking another, thinking one thing and doing another.

6. Value conflicts and lack of unity with their vision.

7. Constantly marinating in regret, always looking toward the past or future, becomes a mental prison. Freedom is in the *now*.

8. Thinking you are your thoughts, not the spiritual being and life force behind mind, consciousness, and thought.

9. Blame, resentment, and excuses.

10. Childhood trauma is creating value conflicts here and now. (See a qualified psychotherapist - I do, it helps.)

"Our thoughts shape us; we become and what we think. When the mind is pure, joy follows like a shadow that never leaves." – Buddha

I can't believe I'm writing this down in a book. Our minds are like tuning forks harmonizing with the frequency we seek to attract.

Making an image in our mind creates a vibration in the physical world and creates the pictures. It literally summons them into physical reality.

Therefore, our thought forms create real shapes.

If you think of electromagnetics, cymatics (shapes of sound on water), and sacred geometry, everything is interconnected. Desire something, form the picture in your mind, be grateful for it, and harmonize with that frequency, and the circumstance will appear in your life. I don't know how much more straightforward to explain it than that.

We are all cosmic manifestation machines with infinite power to mold and shape our reality.

70% of your body is water. 70% of the Earth is water. Water is a liquid crystal and has memory. Everything is energy. Therefore, your thoughts change your vibration and frequency of interacting with your physical reality. The higher your frequency and stronger the positive intention, the more health, vitality, clarity of vision, and faster manifestation.

In quantum physics, you tap into a quantum field that connects all matter, energy, space, and time. Time isn't very well understood. Quantum entanglement describes this interconnectedness, so even if you look at this purely scientifically, there's an Observer Effect when physicists look at a subatomic particle in an experiment, and its position changes based on how they view it. The state and location in space-time of that particle will change based on the observer.

On a macro level, we are all interconnected. How you think about a person impacts them. That's why praying for people, thinking positively, wishing them well, and visualizing better things *for them* is powerful and has created miracles throughout the ages.

If you choose to believe life will be hard, it will. If you doubt a deal will close, it won't. If you question your ability, you'll attract endless realities to prove your doubt.

Feed your faith. Starve your doubt with massive action. (hat tip, John Maxwell)

Believe... Even if you can't see evidence of your vision. It will harden into fact. It will appear real as soon as you go 100% all-in to the pronoia of knowing that the universe is for you, not out to get you. YOU are the block or the supernova blasting a new creative path. If your life isn't going anywhere, build a new reality. Think new thoughts, take new actions, and be grateful for everything in your life.

Per Wallace Wattles, the human who can be thankful for things not yet seen, experienced, acquired, or lived unlocks unlimited power. Before bed, review your day as you'd have liked to have seen it go; be grateful. (Goddard) Visualize the future as now, as already happened (past tense), as current state reality (present tense): then cultivate deep and utter gratitude, joy, and peace. These higher-frequency emotions start to harmonize with the infinite universe and pull you into this reality from the formless into form.

> *"Everything is vibration. Change the frequency and change the channel." – Rhonda Byrne*

Higher frequencies create different electromagnetic waves, changing your vibration and what you attract. The ancients knew this. Boerman even posits that past civilizations could heal people, grow bigger food, levitate objects, and turn lead into gold (alchemy) with specially tuned frequencies.

The universe we are conscious of living in fits within a specific frequency band. Medicinal plants can trigger the pineal gland to open up even higher frequencies. Some can achieve this through music and meditation. Researchers have even found disease lives at certain sonic frequencies, and playing their inverse can eradicate them. Disease = "dis-ease."

Knowing this, why aren't we obsessing over every last thing we want to see and manifest in our lives? Because it's so hard to control those 70,000 daily thoughts. Every technique in this book is dedicated to loosening the grip of that swarm of stinging bees in your head, turning off the white noise, and getting clear, calm, and focused to attract the reality you want. Your mind is literally that powerful. I've seen it to be true in my own life. It's probably all clicking for you now, as unbelievable as it may seem.

Damn, I know. Human beings are genuinely overcomplicating this thing called life. You may have a monkey on your back, a death wish, a weak ego, or too big an ego. You had a hard life? Welcome to humanity: life is suffering. See everything terrible that happened to you as a gift, as an advantage for the wisdom you gained.

Now, start shifting your identity with powerful I AM statements. Right now, reading this, maybe the only string of hope is just, "Justin said this will work." JM said, "I should think this."

When I mentor people and get mentored, I remember something Tony Hughes once told me, "The most powerful thing in this world is believing in another person. When they truly know you believe in them, they're granted permission to achieve their highest vision for themselves."

That's why coaching and mentorship work. When you've got a shattered hollow shell of a person, it's time to pick Humpty Dumpty back up off the floor and rebuild him piece by piece.

Give yourself permission to love, hope, and love yourself again. And above all, you need to make life fun. I'm cracking jokes the entire time I'm cold calling, which has stunned people. I use a neutral tone and consistent humor diffusion; people can't understand how I can maintain that light-heartedness while getting rejected so hard.

I love what I do *because I decided* to love it. If you hate life right now reading this and hate others, you are killing the life force that you are made of. Look under the ocean. Abundance is the natural state of this universe. Not just one fish being born, but millions exploding in fireworks of color.

When you realize that abundance is for you, your birthright, your prophecy, you inherit Eckhart Tolle's *New Earth*. You can harmonize with all the ways you're choking yourself off from the infinite supply. You become a supernova of energy and a magnet for money, which is simply energy. It's merely a yardstick for how much value you deliver as a sales leader, consultant, coach, or entrepreneur.

You become charismatic and pull people and things to you. I was a shy kid if you can believe it. But I was also the class clown and always in the principal's office because my mind was ahead of my body. I talked out of turn and couldn't get along with the other kids or do well with formal schooling. That was kindergarten through 6th grade.

When I caught up to my brain in Middle School, I started producing 20-page papers on Mandela and Gandhi and learning to play guitar like Eric Clapton, whom I later met at 19 at his charity guitar auction. I just bowed when I met him. It was so surreal, and I was suddenly speechless. But I idolized him and Arnold Schwarzenegger all my teens, and then I met them both on the same night.

New success formula (VMA): Vision + mission + action = unstoppable

This chapter should be a huge shot in the arm and inoculate you against the negativity that fills your mind. Learn to love your life and seize the day. Without your health, you have nothing. Without a goal and striving toward it, life is listless. There is no wind in your sails and zero purpose.

I put off living until I turned 40. I mean *living*. I always hedged my bets and had a plan B. I didn't play full out until I realized I had about 14,000 days left if you think of Stoicism and how many 365-day revolutions we get around the sun. I might risk it all, but I wanted to get rich or die trying. I wasn't willing to die with my music still inside me. The cave I feared to enter contained the treasure that I sought, á la Joseph Campbell.

> *"Courage is the greatest virtue because it guarantees all the rest." – Winston Churchill*

My father always said I had "chutzpah the size of mountaintops." Why? Because everything in this book takes boldness. You may say you are shy, introverted, and can't do what I do, but I was once like you. I meet people who feel nerdy or shy around their friends, whereas when gaming or playing sports, they are bold, charismatic, and courageous. You are exhibiting risk-taking, bravery, and boldness somewhere in your life, maybe with siblings or close friends. Introverts are some of the best salespeople as they often deeply listen in ways extroverted types miss.

Tapping into this characteristic of boldness in business and social situations may feel risky, and a coach can help you break that wall. But the truth is, usually, this is a myth and limiting belief. Also, if you are introverted and quiet, and it's just how you love to be, your genius may lie elsewhere in asking smart questions and analyzing problems. *Introvert's Edge,* by Matthew Pollard, proves introverts can still win big in complex enterprise sales or any type of entrepreneurship without sounding like Jordan Belfort.

> *"Vulnerability is not winning or losing; it's having the courage to show up and be seen when we have no control over the outcome. Vulnerability is not weakness; it's our greatest measure of courage." – Brené Brown*

I usually know exactly what to do or where to go because I'm slightly afraid of the decision. It gives me butterflies. Don't expect your goals to manifest if you're not writing them down and reading them aloud as affirmative "I AM" statements on a document, already achieving them in your imagination daily. When in doubt, go with gratitude. If you can take positive risks, feel the fear and do it anyway (Canfield.)

That's my mantra from Jack: FEAR: future events appearing real. 99% of your worries will never happen. In sales, probably the top risk is you will get a "no." They hang up the phone. They reject your offer. No boogie man is hiding in a closet here. There's no great social rejection. You're not going to get fired suddenly.

I'll never forget this classic moment with Jim Mongillo, one of the greatest enterprise sellers ever. I was making a barrage of calls on the Fortune 500 in Manhattan, and someone at a major news media company contacted our CEO, saying, "Chris, call off your dogs." Jim stood me up at the company meeting and said, "Justin got his first complaint, and in my view, he should get promoted." The meaning was not to harass people as a solicitor. The fact is that I was fanatically prospecting where others weren't. Assertiveness is rewarded over passivity in the high-performance sales cultures we build.

Another time, it was 7 pm in San Francisco, and reps were whining, "Nobody answers the phone," mind you, this is the 2016 era. Jim picks up his cell phone and starts dialing the numbers from the CRM. He immediately gets an exec at Spotify and sets a meeting with 150 people watching him in the round during our SKO (Sales Kickoff). It's a true champion moment vividly burned into my brain. "See!"

We aren't succeeding in sales because we aren't taking bold, massive action. We are telling ourselves excuses and buying into the lies of what's possible or impossible. No channels ever die. Everything in sales still works, but it's a sport that requires repetition and discipline so you can get out of your way.

When you MUST succeed, you'll either give up and implode or you will. When your back is against the wall, you will. I interviewed an EVP once and asked what he looks for in reps. He said, "grit and hunger. And even a little debt and a chip on their shoulder." People with massive needs find a way through the tunnel. The proverb, "Necessity is the mother of invention," dates back to Plato.

I can be extremely direct, even blunt. It's not for everyone, but it raises all my results. I powerfully ASK for what I want in all business and social situations. Most people respond well because I'm leading in that scenario. I'll maintain the more powerful frame.

Unlike most other gurus, I do this with humble grace, without force or loudness. But it's how I got here, boldly asking for what I wanted, asking again, asking for referrals, and seeking slammed doors in my face. I "go for the no," not the yes. I'm seeing how many humans I can talk to today, present my offer, and keep moving forward. Babe Ruth was the home run and strikeout King.

A vendor told me once, "Justin, I can vastly improve your close rates." My response was, "I don't want better close rates. I give away 99% of my content for free. I'll powerfully impact the 1% ready to work with me 1:1 on a transformational level." That's why I am one of the top executive coaches in the world. I run an ultra-wide top funnel and am highly selective about my clientele.

The best of the best seek me out. The hungriest who MUST succeed *now* always finds me. A minor league baseball player who had never run an SDR team came to me recently. I had six weeks to teach him everything I knew. ;-)

I was in Northern Idaho at a mobile marketing meetup, and 5 of my former managers were in a circle. My new boss asks, "Is JM the real deal?" They all nodded their head. The description was, "He has the face of an angel and the eyes of a killer." Real closers have a killer instinct. There is no harm here, but they possess an outrageous belief in their ability to get deals done against all obstacles. J.T. described me in this way to the Salesforce higher-ups: "Justin Michael has an incredible threshold for pain." And that meant patience, sticktoitiveness, and the ability to simplify a complex situation as the solver.

Sales is all about politics and diplomacy. I share this not to self-aggrandize but to inspire you to shift away from a wishy-washy, insecure place to understand you have a unique genius you may not have identified or learned to leverage fully. To succeed wildly in sales, we must cultivate our inner power in all business situations.

You are far more powerful than you could ever imagine. I am closing this chapter with two of my favorite David Goggins quotes that sum it up perfectly:

"The vast majority of us are slaves to our minds. Most don't even make the first effort when it comes to mastering their thought process because it's a never-ending chore and impossible to get right every time."

"You have to be willing to go to war with yourself and create a whole new identity."

CHAPTER 6

Create your future from the future (belief)

"It is not in the stars to hold our destiny but in ourselves."

— *Williams Shakespeare*

I found this quote late in life, changing everything. The past is meaningless. You can release your repository of pain at any time. Heaven has no luggage rack; my father used to say [RIP]. You have the here and now and can seize it and build a meaningful life. Take that monkey off your back. Kiss your demons goodbye.

Start to create the future from the future. Break your bad habits at any time. It only takes 21 days to rebuild the neuroplasticity in your brain. If you habitually and obsessively dwell on your victim story and everything terrible that happened and leverage that as an excuse, you are simply building a prison in the present and restricting your abundance going forward.

When I first talk to coaching clients, I always hear, "Well, I can't do that because this [insert brutal thing] happened to me."

"I'm failing because of X, Y, and Z circumstances."

They don't realize they have the entire power of God's life force energy stored in them. They are creators with infinite potential. They've simply kept making the decision often, thousands of times per day, that they can't LIVE. Life is suffering. Learn to find the beauty in it. There's always a lesson, and the result is wisdom. You can become a bigger, more enlightened human *being*.

Oscar Wilde said, "To live is the rarest thing in the world. Most people exist, that is all." Most people spend their lives in a zombie existence. Martin Luther King Jr. once said, "If a man has not found something worth dying for, he is not fit to live." The juxtaposition of these two quotes sums it up. Find your reason to *live*.

> *"Everybody can be great...because anybody can serve. You don't have to have a college degree to serve. You don't have to make your subject and verb agree to serve. You only need a heart full of grace. A soul generated by love."* – MLK

So when people question me, I see greatness in them: "I can't be great. Here are all my excuses." I reply, "It's because you haven't found your heart for service." They fear selling or public speaking, yet they can be humorous with friends, even charismatic. They've made a series of bad decisions that relegated them to the failures in the past. In a healthy human, the failures are just a guidance system helping you get back on course to success. We learn to fail forward.

Trust me, if you're reading this book now and seeking this material, there is greatness in you. I have worked with people who felt like a "lowly SDR" and are currently top enterprise reps at Google.

We are on the path to a default future defined by childhood trauma, memories, and limiting beliefs. But any habit can be changed quickly, and any future reality can be put into your self-image and pulled toward you starting at any time. I believed I would succeed in Silicon Valley, and despite an initial lowball offer, I persevered and worked directly for Sean Parker via an investor connection.

Identity is the whole secret. People don't believe they can earn or go into violent agreement with a threshold on the arbitrary amount of money they think they can make. That's why they must lose - it's subconscious law. The universe says: your wish is my command.

The hedonic treadmill makes us keep with the Joneses. We've all heard about that couple in Manhattan that makes one million dollars a year but has 1.3 million dollars in expenses and goes deeper into debt—like a rat on a wheel, forever racking up more debt where the spending becomes the addiction. I, me, mine: more! The American Dream gets bastardized into superficial materialism in this plastic age. Don't let it define you.

That's why 70% of lottery winners go bankrupt within a few years. They didn't have the identity and mindset to accept this level of wealth. It further confirms that wealth is a state of being, not outward riches you acquire.

When you look into the concept of hedonic adaption, it's friggin' wild. Human beings create homeostasis or a Goldilocks zone of the life they can accept. A $200K earner in sales will do whatever possible to make that income every year. So will a $50K per year earner and a 7-figure earner.

Gay Hendricks called this the "upper limit problem," as we unconsciously set a bar so that if we ever exceed it, we will sabotage ourselves to crash back down. That perfectly sums up the roller coaster that is commissioned sales. People always point to their lack of skills, bad patch (territory), or the comp plan. We are like the golfer blaming the clubs!

You can't just shift instantly from a $200K mindset into a million-dollar one, just as a chain smoker can't just dabble with a nicotine patch and a few fortune cookie slogans. It will take a dramatic internal shift and chronic change in your self-belief to see yourself as worthy of that wealth. Only the processes in this book will rewire your psyche to give you unshakeable belief.

Step one is knowing this: you are holding yourself back - holding yourself in place at your level of income and wealth. No amount of prospecting volume, strategies, or tactical hacks will save you. Courses and cohorts are entertaining, but the forgetting curve will sink you unless you practice daily—my classic advice: don't learn to heli-ski from a manual. The game of life is a full-contact sport. It's an unforgiving and unrelenting challenge for everyone. Especially if you haven't mastered your mind yet and your thoughts are ruling you.

95% of your waking operations are subconscious; you will always do what is necessary to adapt to your level. Let's work together to break through that. Hence, I've gone so hard on this book in the direction of practical self-suggestion exercises to shatter this force shield of self-imposed mediocrity we all don't realize we create.

Our brains are wired to prioritize survival over thriving. Fear governs our actions because our brains evolved during the time of hunter-gatherer societies, where predators and warring tribes posed constant threats. Being hyper-aware gave us the illusion of physical safety in those times. However, these instincts don't necessarily serve us in modern life.

A client asked me, "Do I listen to my gut or thoughts, and how do I know the difference?" Your gut always comes from a place of love, prosperity, and building you up. The subconscious is tricky because you often think from it and don't realize it.

Why are you blocked? You are not grateful. Gratitude was the longest chapter in Wallace Wattle's *Science of Getting Rich*. I grew up charmed with a loving family, but I was never appreciative enough. I got to sing on stage with Kenny Loggins at 21, but I focused on my lack of a Grammy Award. I got to work for my dream companies like Salesforce and LinkedIn, but I fixated on the next mountain: becoming a CRO.

If you wonder why you are not manifesting your greatest dreams, a simple lack of gratitude is likely the first culprit.

How do you shift your identity from being? People get stuck at the willpower level and try to muscle their minds into thinking positively. The issue is they can't truly impact their true root identity and limiting beliefs with occasional goal setting. Sellers tend to maintain a specific income level and even be able to close or "not close" a particular kind of deal. They hold themselves back from receiving a promotion. I hear this all the time, "I suck at opening," or "I suck at closing." And so it shall be your experience.

When your internal *being* is off, deals blow up, jobs go South, relationship conflicts arise, and we often attract an adverse outcome in business almost mysteriously. Does anyone have that friend who seems like a character in the comic strip, *Charlie Brown*? "Bad luck" or "bad things happen in threes" are phenomena the law of attraction (LOA) explains, whereby cosmically, multiple misfortunes find us simultaneously.

When you strengthen your frame and who you are being, you show up differently, you set a new tone, and you are seen as a leader. Advancing you is a foregone conclusion by leadership. You change internally, the world changes around you, reacts differently, and opportunities emerge from the woodwork.

Who am I? You must ask this question, clarify your answers, and write it down. When you formulate this core conception of yourself, it must be holistic, reflecting your highest self. You started this life as a baby with unlimited potential. As you grew, you had to learn to stay affixed to that post by a tiny little string, but your inner baby elephant is now 7 tons and could snap the line instantly. So why don't you? Wouldn't today be a good time to change the rest of your life?

Now, you need to unlearn what's holding you back. Here are a few affirmations that I love. Feel free to try them on for size. I am taking some inspiration from the work of T. Harv Eker.

"I am a genius, and I apply my wisdom." – Dr. John Demartini

"I am joyfully driving my new red Porsche Carrera convertible down the Pacific Coast Highway in Malibu." – Jack Canfield

"I am enjoying living in my beautiful beachfront villa on the Ka'anapali coast of Maui or somewhere better." – Jack Canfield (He made this one happen! See how *specific* it is.)

"I am whole, perfect, confident, strong, loving, harmonious and happy." – Rhonda Byrne

"I am so happy and grateful now that money comes to me in increasing quantities through multiple sources on a continuous basis." – Bob Proctor

Wild side note from the late, great Bob: "You don't just say that once or twice, you've got to repeat that a thousand time a day, every day, for 90 days and you'll start to change your whole concept about money.

"Everything goes right for me."

"I am a magnet for money."

"Money comes to me easily, freely, and often."

Applied to sales:

"*It's easy for me to build pipeline.*"

"*I'm effortlessly attracting, progressing, and closing big deals.*"

"*I love to prospect.*"

"*I'm constantly opening up new business.*"

"*I have more clients than I know what to do with.*"

"*I am great at selling.*"

"*I am the top salesperson in my company and industry.*"

"*I am powerfully serving my customers; they are renewing and referring new business.*"

"*I've just blown out my number and am ecstatic to go to President's Club.*"

"*I'm always the first person tapped for promotion.*"

"*I love cold calling my prospects.*"

"*I enjoy prospecting, and rejection slides off me like water off a duck's back.*"

"*I'm ecstatic that all the best people want to work with me.*"

Notice the emphasis on gratitude and emotion. Feelings are our emotional guidance system.

You cannot live in fear and expect to lead a prosperous life. You cannot worry constantly and remain healthy. You are giving into your thoughts, believing in paranoia. Flip your life into pronoia. "The universe is plotting to do me good." If you see it that way, thus it shall be. Often, fear is a compass. It's pointing you at the cave you must enter that contains the treasure you seek. (Joseph Campbell) Chronically worrying and fearing becomes an addiction, and it is a vice.

My brain still fears and worries, but I know: "I am not my thoughts." Sometimes, you can say this to yourself out loud. Question your fears and anxieties. Are they true? (Byron Katie) Now that you've let those fall away, get back to focusing on what you want. A higher power designed this realm so that *all you believe is for you*, especially if you give and serve others. You receive abundance in direct proportion to the happiness you desire for others.

If YOU are the main focus of your life, you've missed the bigger meaning of the journey. A selfish orientation of the mind shrinks and attracts lack. You must SHIFT all your energy to focus on serving your prospects, clients, family, friends, and mission.

What do you really, truly want in this life? I always ask this to clients and ask it again. And you should, too. Getting clear about your future is step one of permanent transformation. Most people need to learn their goals, much less write them down. It can NEVER be money. It's never about the money!

Look at Maslow's hierarchy of needs. Self-actualization is the highest state: altruism, philanthropy, and crusading for the greater good. Love and support of our children and family create abundance and prosperity. Helping our parents when they are in their golden years, giving back to our church communities, championing causes we believe in, like fighting child slavery, etc.

What is your why, and what gets you up in the morning?

What would your top wishes be if you had a magical genie? I bring a unique spin on traditional secret LOA teachings to this one. Paint a picture of your ideal world in every detail, but always infuse this with a mission of powerfully serving others. I always make my wishes and prayers for others in my life and for the good of humanity. What I wanted for others ultimately came true for me.

Don't we all want to see a more peaceful planet, vibrating on a higher frequency, where there is more good in the world? People have learned and practiced the law of attraction for millennia and missed the two bigger meanings: Serve others. Translate dreams into action. They've often missed the power of gratitude and the clues to tap into our supernatural subconscious power between waking and sleeping reality, hence this book's mysterious subtitle.

Go with Gratitude exercise:

"When in doubt, go with gratitude." – Kent Ferguson (My headmaster in middle school, 80 years old in 2024)

1. **Be thankful to a higher power** for every last thing in your life that is happening, has happened, and will happen.

2. **Write a massive list** of concrete things you're grateful for.

3. **Analyze where things could have gone wrong** and how they rightly worked out: your better angels. I'll list a few: falling 10 feet off a half pipe, knocking the wind out of my lungs, falling out of a river raft in Class 5 rapids

called the "Devil's Elbow" in Southern Oregon, flipping an ATV off a cliff, and catching my shirt on a branch, getting held down in the barrel of a wave in Zuma beach, having my tire roll off my right-front rim in Malibu, falling off a horse that missed my foot by 1 inch, being in a shootout robbery on Easter Sunday in Costa Rica at a call center I was managing. By the age of 22, I almost died several times, and these near-death close calls I later figured out were God speaking to me, warning me about more immense experiences coming. I needed to change, but I didn't see the signs. I do now!

4. **Take the time to say thank you:** Tell your family, managers, clients, prospects, and friends that you genuinely love and appreciate them. Send little gifts and thank you notes to prospects.

5. **Listen more.** Listening is a kind of gratefulness. It shows curiosity, admiration, and appreciation, which makes you unstoppable in sales. Jay Abraham told a story where the moral is, "If you are the most *interested* person in the world, you are suddenly the most *interesting* person in the world." When you're always waiting for everyone to finish talking all day so you can be brilliant, it's incredibly selfish, kills your sales, and no one feels heard. "He loves to listen to himself talk" is the kiss of death in business. Instead, try saying back or paraphrasing what you hear from people all day for one calendar day. It will have a profound impact on your listening. Be present and be fully there.

Desiderata means "things wanted or needed" in Latin. It's a poem by Max Ehrmann written in 1927 that is in the public domain (so I can share it now), but I found it on a wall in a bar at a very dark time, and it shone like a beacon. Legend has it they discovered it in Old Saint Paul's Church in Baltimore, dated 1692, and they mistakenly thought it was ancient. There's tremendous alignment in these words with everything I've been sharing about your outlook and creating an empowered future. Every time I read it, I cry.

Desiderata

Go placidly amid the noise and the haste,
and remember what peace there may be in silence.

As far as possible, without surrender,
be on good terms with all persons.
Speak your truth quietly and clearly;
and listen to others,
even to the dull and the ignorant;
they too have their story.

Avoid loud and aggressive persons;
they are vexatious to the spirit.

If you compare yourself with others,
you may become vain or bitter,
for always there will be greater and lesser persons than yourself.
Enjoy your achievements as well as your plans.
Keep interested in your own career, however humble;
it is a real possession in the changing fortunes of time.

Exercise caution in your business affairs,
for the world is full of trickery.
But let this not blind you to what virtue there is;
many persons strive for high ideals,

and everywhere life is full of heroism.

Be yourself. Especially do not feign affection.

Neither be cynical about love,

for in the face of all aridity and disenchantment,

it is as perennial as the grass.

Take kindly the counsel of the years,

gracefully surrendering the things of youth.

Nurture strength of spirit to shield you in sudden misfortune.

But do not distress yourself with dark imaginings.

Many fears are born of fatigue and loneliness.

Beyond a wholesome discipline,

be gentle with yourself.

You are a child of the universe

no less than the trees and the stars;

you have a right to be here.

And whether or not it is clear to you,

no doubt the universe is unfolding as it should.

Therefore be at peace with God,

whatever you conceive Him to be.

And whatever your labors and aspirations,

in the noisy confusion of life,

keep peace in your soul.

With all its sham, drudgery, and broken dreams,

it is still a beautiful world.

Be cheerful. Strive to be happy.

– by Max Ehrmann

CHAPTER 7

Develop unshakeable confidence

"A man cannot be comfortable without his own approval."

– Mark Twain

You can get so much more in life if you just ask. I ask thousands of times, whereas others ask a couple. Like Babe Ruth, I'll say it again with gusto: I am the home run king and strikeout king! The stately honey badger personified. And you know what? Rejection doesn't sting anymore. If you have 100% faith in yourself and ask for big things, magical things will happen.

Jack Canfield and Mark Victor Hansen wrote a book called *The Aladdin Factor*. Whether you are leasing a seven series BMW on the last day of the quarter, getting an insane price on earrings for your significant other by showing up with a wad of cash, putting together a moonshot business deal, or going straight to a C-Level or board member to ask for an on-site meeting, I have an infallible motto to gauge what to ask for.

Do two things that scare you before lunch.

Feel your fear and do it anyway; Jack taught me that. When I see a prospect that intimidates me, I reach out regardless. When someone seems like they'll reject me and I feel a twinge of fear or butterflies in the pit of my stomach, I ask anyway. And I ask 4-5 times. Honestly, I get blocked frequently, but what's also awesome? Look at my life. I achieved every last dream I set out to achieve and blew those away. Take this type of inventory on your life.

1. I've met nearly every living hero - the last one on my bucket list is Pat Metheny.

2. My significant other exceeds my wildest dreams.

3. My business thrives in all seasons. I've built multiple companies beyond my wildest imaginings from an innovation standpoint. For example, I co-founded and invested in the 2nd biggest GTM community in the world and the industry's first 1:1 coaching marketplace.

4. Worked for Salesforce and LinkedIn, even after hundreds of rejections

5. Generated 100s of millions of dollars in pipeline for other companies earning 10s of millions

6. I traveled worldwide and lived a lifestyle I couldn't dream of starting as an SDR, living check-to-check.

7. I gained international respect as a thought leader, bestselling author, and executive coach.

8. Received testimonials where I've 4-5X'd the pipeline and income of countless others, changed their lives, turned around failing companies, and opened up new pathways to prosperity for great humans and their families

When I sign on coaching clients, the first thing I ask is: "It's 2025, and you're thinking, Oh shit, I can't believe I accomplished

X, Y, and Z things based on our work together." (hat tip Rich Litvin) This exercise is powerful because it puts them into the state of their wishes fulfilled looking back. They immediately grasp the affirmation process I've been attempting to drill into you throughout this work.

> *"If one advances confidently in the direction of his dreams, and endeavors to live the life which he has imagined, he will meet with a success unexpected in common hours. He will put some things behind, will pass an invisible boundary; new, universal, and more liberal laws will begin to establish themselves around and within him; or the old laws be expanded, and interpreted in his favor in a more liberal sense, and he will live with the license of a higher order of beings." – Henry David Thoreau*

Don't live life in the rearview mirror, but collapse time into the NOW: be happy now. Live the dream now. Know that all life is infinite energy, abundance, and grace for you. You will always get another chance if you have air in your lungs. I am on my 9th life. I was probably on my 9th life by 21 years old.

Back then, I started telemarketing at a call center. I wasn't even ranking on the leaderboard. But within six months, I'd failed enough, so I decided to meet the top reps on the floor and give it one last hurrah. Richard Nuñez seemed to have it all figured out: worked three days a week, made $90K, and went to Vegas every weekend. He was waking up at 3 am Pacific every morning to answer calls from the Eastern Seaboard.

I started waking up at 2:30 am and driving to work for the graveyard shift. David Heinen inspired what I call the "air traffic control" voice and turned me on to Robert Kiyosaki's *Rich Dad Poor Dad*. He had grown up golfing with Tiger Woods and was so good on the phone that he bought a beautiful new condo telemarketing. These guys were only in their early twenties and cleaning up.

Emulating them made me one of the top inside sellers in the company's history out of 10,000 reps. My VP of Sales at the time, J.T., used to march new hires next to my cubicle, and they'd listen as I ran a 9-minute script perfectly. I had it so wired tonally I was unconsciously competent. Because of regulations, I had to read the script verbatim, so my only locus of control was varying my tone. I used to pace juggling a stress ball, taking 50 to 100 credit cards like butter every day. I made $9K in one week and spent it all on a home music studio, but I thought, "This sales career is for me."

I share this story because I made a deliberate decision, "If they could do it, why couldn't I?" Then I emulated the habits of the highest performers and became good friends with them. Within a year, I was promoted to sales management to run and train a 30-person team and supervise 300. Before I even turned 25, I had management experience at scale. I just never knew how I'd apply it. I never realized the secrets of how I'd harnessed my mind, willpower, and vision at that time. It's so clear now.

A friend was involved in SaaS companies and was the president of an e-education company in an incubator, so when I was 26, I started doing some guerilla marketing there. I ordered a stack of used books, probably about 50, and read them from cover to cover—classic authors like Tom Peters, Seth Godin, Robert Cialdini, and Al Ries. Ironically, I was far more self-educated in marketing before entering sales.

Everyone has an edge, even if most don't recognize it; what's yours? Did you laterally shift from another industry? Do you have an aptitude for music, acting, or hip-hop? Perhaps you have a hobby that helps you focus on the finer details. My ability to improvise in jazz has massively applied to B2B sales and writing. Or maybe you just like surfing and, therefore, can make calls better when standing and moving kinesthetically in tune with your clients.

I worked for the same investor for a few years before I got disillusioned with the SoCal scene and moved from the LA area up to SF. Within three months of visualization (read Musifestation.com), I went on to manage 200 nonprofit activism and fundraising campaigns for Causes.com under Sean Parker. From there, the same VP of Sales from the first call center story moved to Silicon Valley.

I had been job hunting there for so long that I had a network of 100 top recruiters. So, I helped him land at an ESP - email service provider - and he later went to ExactTarget in Indianapolis, and that's where he reached out to me and recruited me. Salesforce acquired ET for 2.5B.

Yes, I was recruited in the military sense because I had no idea the level of training I was in for. But, I dutifully shipped with big doe eyes from SF right into the depths of boot camp in Indy. That is where my trainer was the legendary Todd Caponi (author of *The Transparency Sale*). Todd was the first to avoid the mechanical approach and dive deep into the cerebral, evidence-based psychological mindset. His empathetic take on the economics of behavior and decision-making was paramount to my current worldview.

Todd's drills into neuroscience and psychology concerning the customers' decision process deviated so far from the manipulations of the day and into service of the customers' needs. The depth of my codices relies on the ability to chuck traditional sales processes and ensure the correct frame by being certain a prospect does not activate their defenses and distrust.

Nowadays, we know all about being servant-led and the need for transparency that creates trust, bonds, and rapport, but back then, it was wild to be so candid in the sales process. I embedded his conscious and consultative approach in everything I do. I live and breathe the evidence-based trust principles instead of trying to generate any fear-based dynamic for a long-term relationship.

After learning the ropes at Salesforce as a strategic account executive (AE) and growing a solid book of business in the West, I became a sales director. I met Jim Mongillo, a GM with the most influence on the *Combo Prospecting* methodology. A boxer and hockey player, his take-no-prisoners Oracle-style prospecting strategy and confidence set the focus on what I'd do from then on. Within a few short years, I ended up at Swrve and got to work for Jim again—this time as the Regional Vice President (RVP) of Sales in Manhattan.

Tune.com searched for an East Coast resource to open a new office, and I won out from a candidate pool of 300+. I ended up in a cubicle in Chinatown, inventing TRIPLES and codifying what later became the account-based sales development (ABSD) stack-ranking process. (hat tip Lars Nilsson)

I cold-called so aggressively in the mobile marketing industry that everyone who mattered knew my name worldwide. Chief Marketing Officers (CMOs) would call to find out what I was doing, yet they still didn't want to deviate from the tried and true methods to make their team take on cold calls as part of their playbooks. I know it's essential. You should, too. Just do the work.

"Mobile Moments" was an event that eventually had over 700 attendees. They were all packed on a majestic NYC rooftop overlooking a massive naval ship during the day. My highlight was seeing them all there, but how did they get there? Was it a huge marketing push or a fluke? They were coming up the stairwells like sewer rats to attend the event. My event. "Mobile Moments" was a success, but I beamed when the Mobile Marketing Association Chairman was curious.

This was my highlight. I knew he was going to wonder if my team did this. But, when he asked, "How did you do it? Was it a hack, or did you just do the work?" "I just did the work," I replied, smiling. The magic was getting a 63% ratio to show up, but the hard work was making the calls, sitting down, choosing the lists, cleaning the contacts, and dialing.

Yes, over 700 arrived, but I dialed and spoke to 1100 to make that happen. I just did the work dialing. That was my proud achievement and why I beamed when he perked up. Each new person popping out of those stairwells high up in the sky that day cemented my resolve never to let this go and always just do the work. You should, too.

In 2017, I randomly chatted on LinkedIn with Ben Sardella, the first salesperson at NetSuite. He'd built Datanyze (later sold to ZoomInfo) and was building a company with Bryan Franklin, Reid Hoffman's business coach. This single chat was like wildfire, and we must have rapidly exchanged a hundred messages. Next week, they flew me to Silicon Valley to look at me backfilling a co-founder in an autonomous prospecting and AI appointment-setting startup. Does that sound familiar? This was eons before the modern ChatGPT and OpenAI era we experience now.

In a VC apartment, I got up in front of 17 engineers and let it rip on every last prospecting strategy detail I knew for three hours. I got that gig and was suddenly scaling up a business with an incredible global team (including the RevShoppe folks) to 100 concurrent clients. I oversaw all operations from data, targeting, list building, copywriting, and client fulfillment, and I was our resident retention specialist, mitigating churn in an automated triage sheet. (Thank you, Greg Meyer) Demanding 90-hour weeks, I got my first taste of real entrepreneurship.

What was wild about the meeting with the engineers was that they were seeking to map my brain and decisions while prospecting and building it into the AI. I had no idea I'd become a top executive coach at the time. Still, when I learned my CEO, Bryan Franklin, had made tens of millions coaching top leaders like Reid Hoffman, I became fascinated by his demeanor, mindset, and leadership techniques. Two of my favorite quotes are:

"The more enigmatic, the higher the fee."

"We must hold the paradox."

We talked so much about synchronicity. You can see in the story how J.T. appeared in 2001 and again in 2011 as my first VP of Sales doing telemarketing, but then again as the reason I got hired at Salesforce. Yes, the same J.T. who used to march new hires to listen to my nine-minute regulated scripts. Bryan Franklin also took that risk on me running his business at OutboundWorks in 2017 and inspired an entirely new career in 2020, still running into the present as a business coach.

Everything is interconnected; sometimes, when you feel furthest from the path, that's still the path. "Not all those who wander are lost." Tolkien.

Let's take a step back before diving deeper. It is easy to get discouraged by difficulties and start doubting yourself or your methods when deals stall or promises unravel. Trust that those around you will come into play at the right time. In sales, it's not just our journeys tied as one united cloth – our colleagues, managers, prospects, and clients equally dwell in this realm of cause and effect.

When frustrations fuse or missteps make deals unravel, those around us are impacted. The same interconnectedness binds us. So, seeing others also on their winding road, we realize breakdowns aren't aberrations asking us to diverge paths – they are the terrain itself we learn to navigate together. It's those who keep coming back cyclically into your life.

In sales especially, the unpredictable nature of human relationships and the timing of decisions that must align fuels constant uncertainty. However, dealing with complications *is* the profession - not failure at it. Each interaction plays a role in steering us onward. You can see it in my colleagues who come and go and then return like a water wheel rising and falling in cycles.

So, when confrontations arise with prospects, late nights turn fruitless, and politics or personalities cause friction from the top down, these aren't aberrations or indications to wander from our true course. They are the course itself, ever-fluctuating as we learn and grow. It's less about having the perfect maps or playbooks than learning to navigate reality's dynamic systems with the people around you—moments to learn from, steps forward to your vision.

There are no dead ends if we believe everything is connected to a purpose. Those periods feeling most off-track or lost often lead us to the more profound insights necessary for the next mile. They can even help determine our fit for the journey ahead compared to routes forking differently across the mountainous terrain. The terrain is so rugged you feel the tug away from doing the work or making those calls.

Take heart in connecting threads when tangled and guidance in all the indirect signs whenever they seem obscured. Wherever we stand – inquiring, serving, struggling, or succeeding – *is* the trail when traversed consciously and with focus and drive. And, as long as we align actions to purpose, "not all those who wander are lost."

The bottom line is that alignment and identity uplevel your life. My CEO at a crowdsourcing company told me, "You're the best person I've ever seen in 20 years at getting fish to the boat." C-Level after C-Level I worked for told me I had a unique gift with the top funnel and outbound that was savant level. Doug McMillen, my director at Tune.com, championed my promotion to running global sales development. He also was an early believer along with Colin Sutton, who is now at Branch (who acquired my division).

The point is that people in your life will tell you what you're great at, expert at, gifted at, and even genius at. You'll see signs over many years, even decades. But for some reason, we don't listen to the signals and feedback loop presented to us. That's why we must tune in and align with our deepest dreams and what we love to do (so our day-to-day won't feel like work).

Start building up your self-belief, and your identity can permanently change.

In the first two *JMM*™ books, I discuss "market validation" as a quick way to grow your self-esteem. I do believe that is true. Keep your testimonials in a file, send them out often, and re-read them. That's actual living proof of your impact. I wrote this book because I felt we need a deeper self-programming of the supercomputer: your subconscious mind acting on the brain to foster genuine, lasting changes of "being."

I still doubted myself as you read back through my story. I didn't have an ultra-long tenure at roles. I found Big Corporate a bit stifling for my maverick selling style. The early-stage companies I was leading sales in were mercurial, ran out of funding, and blew up a lot. Sometimes, they politely fired me to reduce their burn rate because I made a $200K+ base salary. But I persevered.

One day, my "one day" came. I was 40, sitting in my backyard, and thought, "Wow, half my life could be over. When are you going to get on with the process of greatness? Not becoming: *being*." Something snapped inside me then; the pandemic was hitting, and I had six offers for VP of Sales. I left my last VP of Sales role and started to work freelance (1099) for a couple of those.

My first client was a fitness pop-up gym company backed by Mark Wahlberg. I made 9K. My contact who got me the gig in Australia said, "Justin, you are going to make a million dollars coaching people." I thought, OK, maybe over ten years at this pace. I did the role and couldn't land a single client for three months. Client acquisition for coaching was a "goofy foot surfboard," and nobody wanted it. So, I billed myself as a RevOps expert and quickly scaled up to 40 clients. I hit a $100K day on month four and by month 9, a $200K day. Now, this is common for me.

I built the *Justin Michael Method* operating system to solve the OPENING problem for coaches, consultants, entrepreneurs, new business sellers, player-coach managers, and CROs. You name it. I was taking massive action daily, prospecting anyone who would listen to me. I took on many diverse projects and hired a gifted client, Pat, as my GM.

We failed over; we had more work to deliver than we could handle. I did everything from getting on the phones to selling fractionally for multiple companies (before "fractional" was "cool") to earning $25K creating an internal roadmap white paper on where AI was going for a famous sales AI company. I billed myself as a futurist, hosting multiple podcasts to maximize exposure. I quickly became *overexposed*.

Eventually, I met Julia Nimchinski, who had read *Tech-Powered Sales*, my book with Tony Hughes that became the RevOps bible and international bestseller. She invited me to MC a Cold Calling competition called RevGarage, and I became her Co-Founder on the next project: HYPCCCYCL, which has become the 2nd largest GTM community in B2B. Her next vision has been to create a networked marketplace plus community called Hard Skill Exchange. (Hardskill.Exchange) This revolutionary platform could become the next LinkedIn: the world's first-ever live 1:1 coaching marketplace to upskill any GTM ability.

> *"Those of us that know... KNOW. Nate Stoltenow and I have generated literal $billions from outbound and using JMM™ principles/frameworks." – Andrew D. Henke*

I wrote 17 Codex guides over the last four years and released them open-source on Reddit. Years later, I met people who'd made millions with them personally or by scaling agencies. I had material to coach and train on. I realized I needed to synthesize my techniques from multiple disciplines. The Venn Diagram of life coaching, business consulting, and software sales strategy makes these *JMM™* books a powerful amalgam. I've pulled from these three worlds, broken down the new client acquisition techniques into first principles, AB tested them like crazy, and rebuilt them.

Suppose this is the first book you've read. In that case, I urge you to take the champion mindset you've gleaned from *JMM 3.0* and go back and read *Sales Superpowers (JMM 1.0)* and *Justin Michael 2.0*, which became overnight bestsellers worldwide – containing my entire outbound system.

What is inner seeing, inner knowing, and inner fire? Some people show up in this world with an inherent drive to succeed. There used to be a great show called "Driven" about musicians like Christina Aguilera, who seemingly had an unstoppable vision of where they'd get to from birth. Jim "J.T." Thoeni used to say KTFB when he signed off emails, "Keep the fire burning." I use that one to this day. I always envisioned a better life and that I'd succeed somehow.

Returning to the plastics magnate mentor who told me I was a "communications genius," I had no idea how to monetize it. That's a huge reason I now do intensive *Side Hustle Mastery* workshops to coach people around identifying their unique genius, productizing and monetizing it, and efficiently scaling it up to $5-20K/mo.

Willpower is a double-edged sword. Inner fire is not a physical universe thing. It's an inner knowing of your greatness that is God-given. It is an inner seeing of your manifest destiny as already having happened and being grateful for it. It's about learning to read people and trust your gut. How do you do that?

Take my word for it and apply the knowledge in this book exactly. How did I do that? I met stadiums full of people, did charity fundraising, knocked on doors from bank to bank and shop to shop on Main Street, ran the door of a nightclub, sold shoes, telemarketed, and spent twenty years carrying a bag selling all manner of mobile analytics and marketing automation software.

When working with 20-somethings, I ask them, "Do you want to learn the easy or hard way? Would you like to go through hell and back, be on your 9th life, doubt yourself, and plateau over and over again for 15 to 20 years before you break the million mark? Or make these changes now and take a decade off the journey." I rest my case.

"What is opportunity, and when does it knock? It never knocks. You can wait a whole lifetime, listening, hoping, and you will hear no knocking. None at all. You are opportunity, and you must knock on the door leading to your destiny. You prepare yourself to recognize opportunity, to pursue and seize opportunity as you develop the strength of your personality, and build a self-image with which you are able to live - with your self-respect alive and growing." – Maxwell Maltz

Let's get into troubleshooting & putting it all into practice. By this point in the book, I've repeatedly beaten some messages into you, and I'm probably preaching to the choir. You may think, "I can't do what JM did. I can't move all around the country. I can't afford to take these risks; I'm older. I'm not gifted or a genius at anything. I'm not, I'm not, I'm not." Universe says? "Your wish is my command." You're just restricting your growth. If you're reading these words right now, you must realize you are more qualified than I am.

"The [B2B] business is a cruel and shallow money trench, a long plastic hallway where thieves and pimps run free, and good men die like dogs. There's also a negative side." – Hunter S. Thompson (*original quote says "music business")*

I have no degree, left school at 15 (tested out for a high school diploma), partied my life away in my twenties like everyone else, got into software sales late, worked on commission and got exploited, had no skills, never really polished my resume, never had the right exits, never had anything work out the right way in SaaS, nearly went bankrupt, went into debt, doubted myself, almost quit selling, had several tragedies: deaths in the family, and relationship issues.

I faced my demons. I gave up my resentments. I realized that all business is politics. I became politically masterful in reading and applying the insights from authors like Robert Greene. (Read *50th Law* by 50 Cent and Greene riffing on *48 Laws of Power applied to the real world of the cutthroat street hustlers and the music business.*)

50 took nine shots to the face. He teaches us: "Everything that holds you back and you see as your weakness is your strength. If it doesn't kill you, it's another edge, another facet on the diamond." My father always said, "See every situation from the viewpoint of advantage." One of the greatest points of leverage you can ever get over yourself, which will create your edge in the space, is to flip wherever you're weak into where you're strong.

I'll show you. Do this exercise with me now. Write down a list that looks like mine over the years:

- *I don't have a college degree (2010) >> I've developed street smarts and real-world tactics not taught in any university*

- *I don't have enterprise experience (2011) >> That allowed me to approach enterprise selling in an innovative new way with fresh eyes (now I certify people on JMM™, a wholly original prospecting method I invented from scratch that cuts like a hot knife in the Enterprise)*

- *I don't have long tenures (2015) >> True, but I became the "six years of pipeline in 6 months" top funnel smasher. Many CXOs told me, "I've never met someone that can build high-quality top line faster than you."*

- *I didn't make seven figures a year at Salesforce or Oracle. (2020) >> I help reps crack the code at disruptive early-stage startups (I worked for 13), which poses a unique challenge to cracking into F500 accounts when no one's heard your name.*

And on and on. What's your weakest link? Now flip it and rephrase it as your strength.

"Whether you think you can, or you think you can't – you're right." – Henry Ford

A powerful memory: Speaking of 50 Cent, he has a close relationship with Jimmy Iovine at Interscope, as does Dr. Dre, and when I was 19, I showcased for Jimmy at the Viper Room (Johnny Depp's nightclub where River Phoenix died). I took it as a failure that he passed on my music back then. But now I don't see it that way.

It's just another sign and synchronicity of a young life dedicated to music, band management, A&R, and production that translated into the kind of creativity, improvisation, grit, and work ethic that allowed me to rapidly dominate the software sales industry later on and then teach people how to become experts in all things OUTBOUND. For that gift, I am blessed.

Why are you failing? You are programming yourself to fail. It's a harsh reality but one you must admit to. Once you acknowledge that you are getting in your own way, the cave you fear entering opens up, and the treasure is sparkling. The fire-breathing dragon of your ego, filling you with self-doubt, has flown away.

If you cause conflicts with others, make bitter enemies, or burn many bridges, realize the most brutal truth: you created this internally. Big shout out to Ankush Jain here, "You're not loving yourself enough. If people's negativity can affect you, it's because you let them." It's been a bitter pill to swallow that all the bad and good are coming from within.

As Kush says, "You are love. What else could you possibly be?" There is only fear or love. Choose love. Radiate it. Are other people and circumstances getting you down? Love yourself more, and you will love others, and miracles will begin to occur from the greatest force in the universe. Forgive yourself, and you can forgive others.

Take this on faith and start today. Carl Jung said, "What you resist persists." If you're resistive and hate hearing hard feedback like I do, that's your "cave." That's your limitation and comfort zone, and you must push through it. Make peace with your exes, bullies, trolls, toxic co-workers, bosses, Uncle Sam, taxes, corrupt politicians, Big Brother, the past and the future. Turn off all the fake news meant to shock and agitate you. Make peace inside yourself, and peace and prosperity you shall find.

If you feel "not good enough" or unworthy internally, you'll start to attract the circumstances outwardly with the power of your subconscious mind to manifest that as your reality. That's why that "living document" process is so massive—reading it twice daily, even repeatedly, as it will change you on a heart and soul level.

My client tells me, "I'm struggling with complexity vs. simplicity. I complexify everything and think it's impossible even if I've already mastered it. Being a victim, I can get sympathy. If I dissolve the complexity, I have nowhere to hide. It shows I'm the reason."

I responded, "Anything that is limiting you - is not you. People pleasing, seeking approval as if you're a child again from your parents will keep coming up for you."

He immediately had a breakthrough that he was allowing externalities to impact his happiness instead of understanding it was all coming from within his own mind.

"Follow your bliss, and the universe will open doors where there were only walls." – Joseph Campbell

Music was my talent, but sales and coaching have been my gifts. Gifts come naturally to you, inherently, and this is where I differ from Carol Dweck. We all come into this world with inalienable natural gifts that are such a native state to us we often don't see them. I help people find their true genius, develop unshakeable confidence they CAN monetize it, and create the exact life they want doing what they love. I wasted a decade. Maybe even two so I could find all this stuff. Now you don't have to.

If you block your abundance, you are not giving, loving, and grateful enough. Serve and give to others more. Fall in love with yourself, especially every imperfection. Love your enemies and give up all resentments. Get your entire focus off yourself while you work serving others. When I listen to new clients, it's always "I, I, I, I." And I say, "Don't you see, your relentless self-focus is what's eroding your life and confidence. Shift your focus on serving others, and everything will shift inside you."

The best thing you can do with enemies is wish them well, even pray for them. We can't keep anything rotten in our core without it spilling into every corner of our lives.

"Holding on to anger is like grasping a hot coal with the intent of throwing it at someone else; you are the one who gets burned." – Buddha

We can only BE love. Fear and love are all there is. It's binary. We must constantly choose one to harmonize with a higher frequency and vibration. That is the upward spiral!

When you're in the flow state, cutting a groove, doing what you love that benefits others, time stands still. You could do it all day and completely forget your identity. That's what prospecting became for me. I started to fall in love with talking to strangers. Curiosity unlocked: I was fully there, just listening to their voices.

One of the things you can do to trick your subconscious mind is to do something far out of your comfort zone. "Goggins is a verb," per Andrew Huberman, and David's books are a masterclass on creating daily regimens to strengthen willpower and discipline. Side note: guess who also doesn't drink coffee? ;-)

Per Dr. Andrew Huberman, emerging new neuroscience shows that choosing the hard things builds up the anterior midcingulate cortex, developing resilience and determination.

Tim Joshi has a good take here, "Willpower is the force that keeps you going no matter what. It is applying conscious effort to doing something that you, at some level, DO NOT WANT to do (it is uncomfortable or difficult for you). Willpower is the 'embrace the grind' force of determination that keeps you going even when you are disillusioned or want to quit."

> *"The test of a first-rate intelligence is the ability to hold two opposing ideas in mind at the same time and still retain the ability to function. One should, for example, be able to see that things are hopeless yet be determined to make them otherwise." – F. Scott Fitzgerald*

I challenged the concept of willpower altogether in an earlier chapter, stating that willpower is a myth, so how do we simultaneously hold this paradox of these two contrary ideas in our heads at the same time? "When you visualize, then you materialize. If you've been there in the mind, you'll go there in the body," writes Dr. Dennis Waitley.

See it. Feel it. Act.

Action is the missing link to transform yourself with the law of attraction. But action without vision is folly.

Do two things that scare you by lunch.

Act as if you've achieved your goal and take action from that place. Book a ticket to Chicago and then set 5-10 client meetings using the neighborhood technique. "Hey, I'll randomly be in your area at another client meeting; shall we meet up?" Or, do it in reverse.

Hit up 100 people, letting them know you'll be in town. Once they confirm in advance, only *then* book a flight. Cardone used to do this: just show up in a city unannounced and go after business by knocking on doors. Now that's a bona fide cold call! Strike through your comfort zone and teach your subconscious mind that you are shifting into a new level of awareness. Mike Weinberg calls Southwest Airlines "Saleswest" as it's affordable and has changeable tickets!

When you act congruently to your new identity and being, it quickly reprograms your mind. In Dubai, I got an expensive watch but could easily afford it. It was way out of my comfort zone at the time and even slightly pissed me off. I felt wasteful because frugality with money was programmed into me by my father. But I wanted to be the professional who could create the money to have that watch and make that sum no big deal.

Within two years of getting it, my reality had shifted so much that I regretted not getting an even nicer watch. While this example may seem materialistic, money is energy and a barometer or measuring stick of how much service you provide. When clients complain things are too expensive or your product/service is not worth the ROI, you can now see this limitation in them.

They haven't learned to break their limiting beliefs to invest appropriately in themselves or their companies. They've got a broken relationship with money.

"I have seen a 100% ROI on my investment in Justin's coaching after 20 minutes.

> *Justin opened the Pandora's box for me. He helped me break my limiting beliefs and taught me how to bring my unique gift to others. Justin is the epitome of being a coach: he slows down, listens to me, and truly understands where I need help. Despite his incredible achievements, he never brags and always points out his flaws. I will work with Justin again in the future."*
> *– Christian Krause*

50 Cent Inspired Exercise - see every last weakness as a strength

1. List every weakness you have personally or professionally on paper. E.g., didn't go to college, short stints at jobs, bad at following through with clients over 90 days.

2. Now, rephrase that weakness as a strength. This could sound like: I learned "street smarts" from the "School of Hard Knocks," I'm adaptable, I rapidly get massive results in the funnel, and I offer intensive delivery for quick impact.

3. Next time someone points out a flaw or limitation in you, flip it immediately as a strength. In middle school, my guitar teacher, Marco, was quite overweight, and the kids would tease him. Best response ever, "I may be fat, but you're ugly, and I can go on a diet." He took it in stride and even made the bullies laugh.

CHAPTER 8

Conclusion: Magic is real

"Magic's just science that we don't understand yet."

– Arthur C. Clarke

I wrote this book so you could unlock all your inner superpowers and finally love yourself. The great secret is to be grateful at all times for the life that God gave you and put your focus on serving others.

You must love yourself to love others. You must *be* love, never fear. You must let go of all resentments and forgive everyone and yourself. You can magnetize a new reality toward you from this pure place of higher vibration. You do this by understanding a new distinction:

"I am not my thoughts, mind, or body. I am the formless coming into form."

Practice *Musifestation* exercises 30 minutes a day to align with the universe. We live in a polluted world. The images, sounds, food, and even people can poison our sanity and vitality.

What we focus on grows. If you want more sales, live *from* having "already achieved more sales and being deeply grateful for it." Constantly be thankful for everything great in your life; more will come into it. Believe in things unseen that have yet to happen, as if they're already real. Know in your heart that God is good and everything is for you. That's the baseline of PRONOIA, which attracts abundance into your life even faster.

Paradox: set 10X goals because they are more accessible than 2X incrementality á la Hardy/Sullivan.

Breathe; remember to breathe deep. We are constantly breathing. Breath and thoughts are the fabric of our existence; everything is music: melody and harmony, resonance vs. dissonance. Everything is vibration and energy down to the subatomic level.

You can quantum leap into your future parallel universe in the *now*. Change course at any time; you are the cosmic rudder that can dictate your future, charting your course amongst the stars. You must suck out the poison shackling your soul with auto-suggestion and your new positive mental attitude. Reprogram your subconscious MIND by dedicating time to the deceptively simple exercises in this book.

> *"Those with a mind of their own, and the willpower to control it, can accomplish the impossible." – Brad Turnbull*

Are you ready to effect lasting change by shifting your very *being*? I recommend rereading the book, taking notes, and running through every last exercise to see which ones come most naturally to you. Hypnosis will only make your results come faster. DNA-aligned, Solfeggio-based sacred geometric miracle hertz frequency music (sounding at 528Hz and 432Hz) is the way to speed all of this up. It relaxes your mind to allow your thoughts to clear so you can go into a lucid dreaming meditative state. You can even get Chopin's Nocturnes and Mozart in these unique tunings.

You can draw forth the life you want from imagination, and by shifting your inner identity to a new truth and inner reality, you can pull that created future into the present in real time. It's pretty mystical, but that's how this universe works. Why? Well, that's a topic for yet another book.

The stunning truth about success is we all hold ourselves back. We all sabotage ourselves. Our conscious awareness is only 5% of our mind, while subconscious forces control 95% beyond our waking reality. In that case, it's no wonder we often feel doomed like Sisyphus, performing the same cyclical manifestation and experiencing the same karma repeatedly in our jobs, romantic relationships, and financial conditions.

You can learn NLP or get hypnotized to speed these processes up, but that wasn't practical for me. Listening to music tuned to various frequencies helped me relax into Alpha/Theta states as a stargate portal to time travel from my Beta-coffee-addicted life. I could finally visualize and go into a lucid dream state where I could reprogram my subconscious mind, therefore manifesting a new reality. Figure out which one of the nine ancient Solfeggios makes you feel best at a specific point across the hertz (Hz) spectrum.

Musifestation works, and the people I've shared it with over the last decade have realized tremendous results.

Resistance to change! You will come up with a million and one excuses why this method is too "woo woo" and won't work. It's too new age. It's too spiritual. But looking into modern neuroscience, the "entanglement" and "observer effect" concepts in quantum mechanics, and the reticular activating system's (RAS) power, you'll see hard science supporting everything I've written in this controversial book.

My aim is for this writing to have a profound positive impact on your mental health. That's been the missing link and Achilles heel of sales methodology's past. In my view, it's not about taking a special "mental health" day; it's about fine-tuning your mind every waking hour as a constant discipline. In a single moment, your life can change forever. Sometimes, it's something so fundamental, simply gaining an understanding or resolving a misunderstanding.

> *"You can do anything when you rewire your brain, believe anything is possible, and you control the meaning of what happens in your life." – Tony Robbins*

Do you want to become a better seller? Be. That. Now.

Shift your identity to a new consciousness, and state boldly to yourself: "I am the real timer in the world." "I am the top seller in my industry." "I am the top seller in my company." But emphasize serving your customers. "I am transforming my clients' businesses and lives for the better."

Know that you are great and were put on this earth to manifest prosperity beyond your wildest dreams. Your potential is just like mine: infinite. You only believe the lie your subconscious mind tells you that you're not worthy, not good enough.

I spent 15 years beating myself up mentally and coming up with reasons and excuses from my past that justified why I couldn't succeed wildly. It's sick and twisted, but maybe we even get some satisfaction from failing. I guarantee you it's better to live a comfortable life than seek out sympathy.

You may read this book and return to your old ways and comfort zone. Then reread it. Get up right now and *GO* do something! The antidote to your struggle is ACTION. Remember, you can never get enough of what you don't want.

I am my worst enemy, and it's no different than you. I tell my clients, "Love yourself more, build yourself up from the inside, and find the champion within." That's how you live your legend like Rocky Balboa. That belief is the acorn that will become an oak tree and soon a forest of "winning" and self-discovery. You will begin to trust yourself and listen to your inner voice.

How many messed up situations have you ended up in where you just wished you'd listened to that voice inside in the first 3 seconds that foreshadowed everything you needed to know? Make that voice louder, clearer, and stronger through stillness and meditation. Learn to listen to God.

You will have haters. 1 in 1,000 people will hate you as you shine bright and put yourself out there. That's a positive sign in a world of sheeple going with the current as you swim up it. "Success is the greatest revenge," per Sinatra. Put your head down and stay "independent of the good opinion of others," as Maslow & Dyer stated.

Kill off people pleasing and seeking approval from others. Quit taking selfies and talking about what you will do. Be awesome under the cover of darkness, and let people discover it organically afterward.

> *"Two roads diverged in a wood, and I— I took the one less traveled by, And that has made all the difference."*
> *– Robert Frost*

Something snapped in me around 40. It was time to do two things. One, silence my greatest fear: I wouldn't live up to the potential everyone saw in me, from family to teachers to managers. Two: I finally put down the monkey on my back and thrived. Every last thing I was scared of, I immediately did.

My twenties were the lost decade. My thirties were the life I thought I should live. My forties are life on my own terms. If I only knew now, then. "Shoulda, woulda, coulda – didn't." Regret is pointless.

In decade three, I courageously moved cities, applied to companies I never thought I'd get hired for, and contributed to bestselling books.

In decade four, I found my original voice as an author and shared it with the world. I launched and scaled an international consultancy. I endlessly put myself out there and got thousands of "Nos." I co-founded a GTM agency and tech startup.

Whenever I thought it would be hard, I chased the discomfort and exited my comfort zone. I used the principles in this book to make people, clients, and opportunities pursue me.

One of my massive purposes is to cut 15 years off your journey so you don't have to plateau making lateral moves. My coaching is about helping people find their true selves. Why not live out your true goal in the prime of your life? Humans usually put off what they truly want to do until a distant rainy day. It baffles me, and I wanted to know why. Self-sabotage is our trauma blocking us.

Some of you are over 40. They told you, "You can't become an entrepreneur. It's too late." They put you out to pasture. Also, not true. I've run into 80-year-olds lately, like Arnie, who are vital. Age is a state of mind.

Clifford-Lewis's recent research with Javier Miranda of the U.S. Census Bureau and Pierre Azoulay of MIT found "that the average age of the most successful entrepreneurs is 45."

I became the garden. It was a single decision, followed by another and another.

Building momentum, I eventually went through the metamorphosis to become a butterfly and then attracted the butterflies to me, as you will now.

Vision without action is futile.

A high work ethic often creates the "busy fool" syndrome. We must endeavor to work smarter, not harder. And the hardest work is mental. Take all the mindset mojo you learned in *JMM 3.0* and execute from that new place of being as you take radical, massive action based on *JMM 1.0* and *2.0* (the most profound client acquisition system ever built).

Go with God's life force energy and relentlessly get back off the mat when knocked down and crusade to your dreams. Maintain an "in-tune" mind, purpose, and sole focus, and put these pictures in your head at all times, before bed, before you sleep, in the waking hours, habit stacking when you run, play sports, and work out.

Believe in the unseen, new you, new reality, even when everything around you shows the opposite. That is the unlimited power and complete secret to living on this plain, whatever forces mysteriously govern it. I believed I'd pass seven figures for 20 years, and then I did. I never once doubted it deep down because I knew I could. If others could do it, why couldn't I? Do you know you can? I believe you can.

My clients get outrageous results - 5Xing income, often surpassing seven figures. Some are building 8 figure businesses now using these principles. If you want to transform your life, earn millions, get promoted, launch a side hustle, sculpt the most confident version of yourself, break free from the shackles of your past, and completely shift your sense of being, identity, and reality, I can help you.

Morpheus: "This is your last chance. After this, there is no turning back. You take the blue pill - the story ends; you wake up in your bed and believe whatever you want to believe. You take the red pill - and you stay in Wonderland, and I show you how deep the rabbit hole goes." (The Matrix)

You are NOT your story. Let's write a new one. Let's create the future from the future. And for that, again, I thank Werner Erhard in closing for this simple distinction.

The NOW is infinite. Build a new version of your reality right now.

Contrary to everything we hear about hiring humans, your past does not dictate your future. Mine certainly did not. Thank God.

Your thoughts are infinite. Your feelings tell you where you're going.

Choose your own adventure. Choose LOVE.

By changing who you are being in any situation, you can manifest a new reality.

Luke Shalom did. He's turning just 29. My star protegé changed his mindset, took action, and attracted a quarter million dollars rapidly into his life, investing in my coaching twice:

> *"Hit 160% quota*
>
> *Had my first five-figure profit month*
>
> *You told me to go all in, went all in*

Scaled to $10K MRR

Kept pushing with the 4th Frame; we hit $20K MRR

Then we finished the year closing $250K of contracts."

"Perhaps we shall learn, as we pass through this age, that the 'other self' is more powerful than the physical self we see when we look into a mirror." – Napoleon Hill

Thanks for making me, Mom.

Here's her take, forever young at 73: "The law of attraction works because it is a *law*. This is the way the universe works. When you raise your vibration by feeling better, having more fun, being more productive, etc.... You will attract energies and things at that same higher vibration. I am having great success up-leveling my life using the law of attraction."

About The Author

Justin Michael is a world-record-breaking, outbound sales maven who has arguably built the deepest client acquisition methodology of all time: the Justin Michael Method (*JMM*™). It's driven over 1B in pipeline for 200+ startups he's advised and over 25K reps, 1K of which he's personally coached. With 20+ years in sales, ex-Salesforce, and LinkedIn, Justin is the global authority on AI-based outbound prospecting alongside legends like Aaron Ross, Josh Braun, and Mark Roberge. His counterintuitive, mobile-responsive, neuroscience-backed visual prospecting methodology made him a million-dollar earner and helped countless startups scale past ten million dollars ARR. His clients frequently 2-5X their pipeline and income, consistently getting promoted within six months. Justin is the bestselling author of "Sales Superpowers" and "Tech-Powered Sales," which proved that over 75% of top funnel can be automated by raising your technology quotient (TQ). He lives in Los Angeles, California, advising top SaaS technology CROs and teams on bleeding-edge revenue models.

Learn more at SalesSuperpowers.com.

Made in United States
Troutdale, OR
05/29/2024

20208202R10108